Humanism
and
Jewish American Drama

Humanism
and
Jewish American Drama

D. Venkateswarlu

PRESTIGE

Published by
Prestige Books
3/28, East Patel Nagar, New Delhi 110 008
in association with
Indian Society for Commonwealth Studies
New Delhi

ISBN 81-85218-19-6

Jacket design by
3-A Corporation
New Delhi 110 002

Phototypesetting by
data culture
New Delhi 110 065
Ph. 6431070

Printed at
Mehra Offset Press
New Delhi 110 002

Contents

FOREWORD

When I first read it, Mr. Venkateswarlu's book struck me as being almost as exotic as his subject must have seemed to himself when he approached it. The cause of this initial impression, I came to feel later on, was the style in which the writer expressed himself, and, however important that might be, there was something still more so: the solidity of the matter he had to express. Three things continue to impress me: the scope of the subject his intellectual ambition has prompted him to address, the extent of the information he has amassed about it, and the degree of his sympathetic identification with the people—not American Jews in particular but the historical Jews of the world generally—whose modern dramatic literature he has undertaken to study. He seems to me to have achieved a proper balance of objectivity and subjectivity in his assessment of his subject, and his wide survey, which ranges from the familiar to the less familiar, should have value for those seeking an introduction to his subject and is not without interest for those who know a good deal about it. It is quite clear, in the end, how much labor—under conditions hardly favorable to such research—must have gone into the assimilation of so much material, and the writer has laid a basis for further work along the same lines.

Department of English
Brandeis University
Massachusetts

MILTON HINDUS

For

Rabbi S.S. Koder,
Eva and Milton Hindus,
and the Brandeis Community

Preface

This book, in more ways than one, had to be written after all. Being brought up on the Anglo-Saxon projections of the Jew in English literature programme here and abroad, I began to view the Jew, at least initially, from purely ideological ambience. In a way, it seems to me, that all literature is an act of such perceptions or propagations. The need to discuss literature necessarily in an apolitical context, without doubt, is a gesture of vested interest—to say the least. If anything, I have certainly survived these prejudices. The emergence of the Jew from a victimized status of a Shylock to an authentic metaphor of modern man is riddled with demystified angles of vision, as this work attempts to argue in the following pages. Although it started as an academic adventure, it soon began to emerge as a major influence in my literary and socio-political reappraisals.

No such enquiry is possible without a generous help from numerous sources that have shaped my views and arguments. Inevitably, thanks are due to many people. Dr. Isaac Sequeira has gone through the draft at various stages of its preparation. I have benefitted greatly from his comments and suggestions. My teachers at Brandeis University have taken special interest in my work especially Prof. Milton Hindus. Prof. Leon A. Jick, my teacher and advisor, Prof. Eugene Goodheart, Prof. Marshal Sklare, Prof. Marvin Fox and others on the faculty of the Near Eastern and Judaic Studies Department have helped in widening my perceptions. My indebtedness to the Weidener Library of Harvard University is immense. Prof. Harold Fisch's talks on Hebrew theology have been especially helpful.

Rabbi S.S. Koder has been kind and generous to me in many

ways. Not only did he allow me to consult his precious library but also enlightened me on Talmudic matters. I enjoyed his hospitality for days—and on many occasions.

Gladys, Lily and Elias, affectionately welcomed my stay with them. Similarly Eva Hindus and Myra gave me a sense of family in Boston. The dedication of this book to them is a small token of gratitude and affection. Dr. Jerry Prillman, Dr. Nathan Katz and, my dear friend, Dr. Robert Hamburger deserve a special mention here. The Brandeis community has given me the necessary intellectual stimulation that will remain with me forever.

Introduction

Humanism on Trial: The Demythification of a Stereotype

Before one makes an attempt to analyze various social, cultural, political and religious aspects of Jewish stereotypes, created by non-Jews, it is instructive to review the cognitive implications of the two key terms which figure prominently in this chapter and, in fact, in this book itself namely: humanism and stereotype. Since these terms are used in many contexts and sometimes, as critics say, even irresponsibly, it is safer to circumscribe the scope in which these terms are used here to enable us to have a clearer perspective. Humanism, as a term, gained currency from the Renaissance which emphasized the need to have a man-centered attitude to life. The Greek and Roman classical writers contrasted human and bestial qualities on the one hand and the human and divine on the other, only to underline the pathetic side of man especially his mutability and fallibility whereas medieval Christianity felt that man's life on earth has relevance in so far as it strives to prepare itself to the life after death which eventually became a point of disagreement among the Renaissance writers and "it was against this belittling of his natural condition that the humanists of the Renaissance asserted the intrinsic value of man's life before death and the greatness of his potentialities."[1] Thus man strove to become what Protagoras had in mind for him that he is the measure of all things. With the inevitable decline of religious influence, the Renaissance viewpoint attracted favourable attention which continues to find sympathizers and followers even to this day in various forms and under various ideologies. Whatever may be the genesis of this term, today humanism is considered, in a general perspective, to be "the philosophical and literary movement which originated in Italy in the second half of the fourteenth century and diffused into the other countries of Europe, coming to contribute one of the factors of modern culture. Humanism is also any philosophy which recognizes the value or dignity of man and makes him the measure of all things or somehow takes human nature, its limits, or its interests as its theme.''[2] Humanists emphasized the conceptual relevance of freedom, naturalism (in the sense, that man is a part of nature and cannot be abstracted from it), historical perspectives (return to antiquity), religious tolerance and science. Thus humanism has come to signify many schools of thought. In fact, the *Encyclopedia of Philosophy* states that the term encompasses the four doctrines:

1. Communism, in that it could abolish man's alienation from himself, which is a product of private property and capitalistic society.
2. Pragmatism, because of its anthropo-centric view, as Protagoras did, makes man ''the measure of all things.''
3. Personalism (also called spiritualism) which affirms man's capacity to contemplate the eternal truth or, in general, to enter into a relationship with transcendental reality.
4. Existentialism, which affirms that ''there is no other universe than the human universe, the universe of human subjectivity.''[3]

These considerations, in turn, enabled many theoretical critics to conveniently take the term and attach it to their sometimes diametrically opposite epithets. Though primarily it had a definite meaning in the Renaissance, humanism seems to have accommodated many features of modern thought, or to put it more truthfully, most of the modern concepts, schools of thought, and movements seem to have declared themselves humanistic. Consequently, the epithet humanism has acquired many telling adjectives as in the following: Marxist humanism, liberal humanism, New Humanism, religious humanism, atheistic humanism, scientific humanism, absurd humanism, ethical humanism, radical humanism and existential humanism. And certainly there could be many more. Despite sharp differences on many levels, one thing can be stated without running into conceptual controversies: all these concepts single-mindedly dedicate their rhetoric towards the welfare of man or exclusively concern themselves with various aspects of man. In this sense, they are extensions of Renaissance humanism in more ways than one.

Bogged down by a plethora of these terms, a critic wonders if it is possible to define humanism at all. Vaan Praag goes on to state: "Humanism is what it is through existential values. It is bound up with emotion and evaluations. It is a moral conviction rather than a theoretical speculation. Therefore it is more suited for a clarifying description than for an unambiguous definition."[4] In the same book edited by Paul Kurtz, where this article appears, H.J. Blackham resents any definition of humanism because epithets like, 'ethical,' 'scientific,' 'religious' are used as exclusive terms which suggest an exclusion of other aspects of man. Finally, he says: "Abstractly, then, Humanism is a concept of man focussed upon programme for humanity. Concretely, it is my idea of, and my commitment to, my part in that programme, which includes not least that is in my own hands."[5]

Considering the problems one faces with these terms, the aforementioned statement seems to be justified for there are even ideological conflicts between one term and another as in religious humanism and atheistic humanism; liberal humanism and Marxist or socialist or radical humanism; and ethical or moral humanism and absurd or existential humanism. Many of the modern social and philosophical concepts and movements proclaim that they are humanistic though they have to settle their quarrels with others and oftentimes rival ideological movements who have made similar claims to that effect. What is common in these divergent ideologies with their humanist claims is that they have tried to interpret human concerns and have made a social, political or philosophical programme for humanity, according to their ideological stances. Though there are differences, their concern for humanity in various contexts are laudable, for even in their differences, they have not ignored human welfare and the problems faced by humanity. It is this contribution from various ideologies that gains attention in this book. Hence, Jewish radicalism and Hebrew scriptural humanism are also classified as humanistic. Humanism, in this sense, encompasses the concern for man as against the annihilating environmental forces, be they political, social, religious or cultural. Thus, the persecution of the Jew, the Christian or non-Jewish creations of Jewish stereotypes, without attempting to know about the actuality of Jewish life and the perpetual struggles the Jews had to wage against the unfounded myths of themselves, become a humanistic concern. It is in this sense, "humanism on trial" is intended.

This leaves us with another clarification regarding the term, stereotype, which is largely confusing and, if we are to believe the social scientists, has been used consistently in an ambiguous manner. From the technology of printing where it originated, this term has travelled in astonishing conceptual guises. The original meaning of the word in printing is precisely this: "A body of type is set up; then a mould is made from this type, and a solid metal plate is the stereotype."[6] In due course of time the adjective stereotype came to mean "hackneyed," "trite," or "mechanically repeated." The word as a social concept has been used by Walter Lippmann, an American journalist, with a special social implication in his book *Public Opinion* (1922). In this book a chapter has been allotted to a discussion of stereotype as a social concept. While analyzing social stereotypes Lippmann says:

> Each of us lives and works on a small part of the earth's surface, moves in a small circle, and of their acquaintances, knows only a few intimately. Of any public event that has wide effects, we see at best only a phase, and an aspect. This is as true of the eminent insiders who draft treatises, make laws, and issue orders, as it is of those who have treatises framed for them, laws promulgated to them, orders given at them. Inevitably our opinions cover bigger space, a longer reach of time, a greater number of things, than we can directly observe. They have, therefore,to be pieced together out of what others have reported and what we can imagine.[7]

Since we do not know fully about many matters, we begin to base our judgements on the basis of available information. As time goes on, these few bits of knowledge become authentic for us, as a consequence of which we do not believe anything that does not conform to the already established sources of our judgement. These, in turn, become stereotypes. Lippmann uses this term as a social concept. These stereotypes influence us to a large extent. Lippmann says: "The subtlest and most pervasive influences are those which create and maintain the repertory of stereotypes. We are told about the world before we see it. We imagine most things before we experience them. And those preconceptions, unless education has made us acutely aware, govern deeply, the whole process of perception."[8] It would be revealing to discuss Jewish stereotypes of prejudices in this light. However, Lippmann deals with this issue in terms of political decision-making which, as he says, is often based on stereotypical assumptions. John Harding sums up the implications of stereotype: (1) It is simple rather than complex or differentiated; (2) it is erroneous rather than accurate; (3) it can be acquired second-hand rather than through direct experience; and (4) it is resistant to modification by new experience."[9] He hastens to say that these characteristics may vary independently and are not necessarily, positively correlated. Stereotype is also synonymously used as a group concept. Jewish stereotypes are discussed largely according to these assumptions. In fact, the American Jewish committee organized empirical research, carried out by luminaries of social science and philosophy like T. W. Adorno and Bruno Bettelheim who delved deep into the subject to perceive the reasons for stereotypes of prejudice. Adorno along with others published *The Authoritarian Personality* (1950) and Bruno Bettelheim wrote a book entitled *Social Change and Prejudice* (1950). In both these books Jewish stereotypes are discussed extensively. Adorno, talking about the stereotypical notion of non-Jews regarding Jews, comments; "The fact that people make general statements about 'the Jew,' when the Jews are actually so heterogeneous—belong to every socio-economic class and represent every degree of assimilation—is vivid evidence of this irrationality.''[10]

Adorno and Bettelheim try to argue against the irrational assumptions of Jewish stereotypes which have been encouraged by certain people or establishments for their social, political and religious reasons. The perpetuation of stereotypes continues, taking sustenance from the atmosphere of prejudice which makes them reluctant to test whether their attitudes are valid or justifiable by taking reality into consideration. In the case of anti-Semitism this proved to be the essential myth. Since literature is essentially a product of society, the social pattern, not the least its deeply-felt notions and prejudices, impinge either consciously or unwittingly on the creative process. They, in turn, seem to function as propàganda, once the artistic piece is consumed by readers or art-lovers. The interaction between society and art produced an extended myth which could be perceived even in the best of literatures. The fact that Shakespeare himself is not safe from this, is enough proof to conclude how irresistible these social prejudices are. Writing about the lack of reality-testing, Bettelheim gave a psychological viewpoint in this connection:

> Such a limited account of reality-testing, however, did not seem to be available to strongly biased individuals. Their intolerance signified a much stronger underlying need for hostile discharges which had to be totally predicted through real experiences. In these cases stereotypes became their defense, and since the pretension of reality-testing had to be maintained, the Jew was no longer tested against reality. On the contrary, instead of testing whether a Jew, or the majority of Jews, conformed to the stereotyped picture of the Jew which was used to justify anti-Semitism, the reverse procedure takes place. Whoever fitted the stereotyped pictures of the Jew was accepted as such, and used to support the validity of the stereotype.[11]

This account gives a rough picture of what sustains these stereotypes. Having surveyed the genesis of stereotypes with special reference to the Jews, we now come to a state where literary responses can be assessed with this background in mind. The history of the Shylock-stereotype, to speak of one major stereotype of prejudice, unquestionably necessitates such a long analysis of the term and its social and psychological readings. With these views as framework, the image of the Jew in drama can be analyzed with a fleeting overview.

Arnold Wesker wrote *The Merchant* in 1973 nearly four centuries after Shakespeare's version of Shylock. In this play, he re-told the story of Shylock but this time he is not a money-grubbing, or devilish Jew. Shylock is liberated from the prejudicial confinements of Shakespeare's *The Merchant of Venice* (1596). Wesker is intrigued when even the ardent Jews try to make comments in favour of Shakespeare on the portrayal of a 'sympathetic' Jew considering the atmosphere of the Elizabethan society. Wesker feels that characters in a play are not chosen arbitrarily. They represent the playwright's intention of certain characteristics and "The Jew in Shakespeare's play is meant to embody what he wishes to despise."[12] If Shylock has those sympathetic words wherein he pleads for his humanity, it speaks volumes for Shakespeare's dramatic instinct, because this portrayal makes him more human than portrayals of Jews on the stage upto that time. It also makes, as Wesker rightly feels, anti-Semitism more dignified than it used to be. Watching this play in the National Theatre, Wesker was horrified at the play's "irredeemable anti-Semitism,"[13] because he never could recognize a Jew in real life with this vengeful attitude. He concludes: "A director of Hungarian origin told me he'd seen a production in war-time Hungary where the play's anti-Semitic aspects were inevitably exploited to the hilt. I can't help feeling there's a certain honesty to such a production, and I would like to think Shakespeare today would be ashamed of his contribution to the world's image of that poor old battered race."[14] This is the reaction of a Post-Holocaust Jew and one cannot discount this response if Shakespeare's play is analyzed scrupulously. While talking about the term stereotype, mention has already been made of the fact that the reluctance to reality-testing is one of the reasons why the stereotypes of prejudice continue to play a role. In the case of Shakespeare, one may argue that he is a practical dramatist and not a social historian to check up the sources so responsibly and since he is conscious of public taste, he gave what they can possibly appreciate. How far this argument is commendable, can be understood if one looks at some of the aspects of the play where one can see the age-old prejudices.

Although *The Merchant of Venice* has many thematic levels, one of the most important aspects appears to be the religious one: the contrast between a good and benevolent Christian and a villainous and demonic Jew. In the conversation between Shylock and Antonio (Act One, Scene III), Antonio says: "The devil can cite Scripture for his purpose." (37) He says in the same context that when the Hebrew turns Christian, he tends to behave with kindness towards others. Now, let us see what others have to say about him. Lancelot, Shylock's servant, says that Shylock is "a kind of devil," "the Jew is the very devil incarnate," "the friend" (69) and "I am a Jew, if I serve the Jew any longer." (105) Here he makes a difference between Christian and the Jew as a master. For Lorenzo, Shylock is "a faithless" person. (89) Solania feels that he should say 'amen' often because the devil, in the likeness of the Jew Shylock, may not cross his path. Similarly all the characters make unsympathetic comments on Shylock, the Jew. The court scene provides a scathing attack on Shylock and the things he represents. What is significant in this controversy is the generalization. It is never the individual Jew but a generalization and the stigma is attributed to the entire race whereas Antonio is an individual though he represents the benevolence of a good Christian. In fact, the popular sentiments have been given a new twist in this play. For instance, when Shylock is asked to change his mind regarding the bond executed, he adamantly refuses and says: "My deeds upon my head" (179) thus reminding the story of crucifixion and the Jewish contribution to it, at the time when Pontius Pilate washes his hands putting the entire blame on the Jews and they wholeheartedly accepting it. The critics who say that Shylock has been given a chance to express his humanity often forget the emotional upsurge such words can bring about in the masses. Coming back to the theory of the devilish Jew, it is even more revealing that Shakespeare makes effective use of popular prejudices. This is also justified by certain people on the pretext that since Shakespeare is a practical dramatist, he knew what works with the masses and what does not. This typical absolution of Shakespeare cannot underwrite the fact that the accumulated prejudices have done their damage. Wesker's response is totally justified and redeemingly enough he retold Shylock's story. Joshua Trachtenberg, who has done an extensive study on the aspect of the devil and the Jew, believes that this attitude is the product of the medieval concept of the Jew, not least influenced by the rationale of the Gospels, Jewish non-conformism and economic competition. This medieval creation of the Jew, "outlined by early Christian theology and ultimately puffed out to impossible proportions, supplanted the real Jew in the medieval mind, until that real Jew to all intents and purposes ceased to exist. The Only Jew whom the medieval Christian recognized was a figment of the imagination."[15] These misconceptions crept on even to the recent times in the form of Jewish stereotypes.

Shylock's presentation on the stage cast an unusual interest in his character and many historians, as Jacob Marcus points, tried to find a historical basis for such a portrayal only to find that it is an old folk-tale. Jacob Marcus continues: "The oldest known European version of the tale appeared in Latin, in Lorrain, sometime before 1200. In this work, Dolopathos the villain is not a Jew, but a revengeful slave."[16] The villainous Jew appears in the English *Cursor Mundi*, about 1290. But there is no evidence to confirm that Shakespeare's source is this play. There is an Italian version of the revengeful Jew presented in Giovanni Fiorentino's *Il Pecorone* (circa 1378). Marcus also says that Shakespeare is probably inspired to write this play "because of the public interest in the trial and execution in 1594, of the Marrano physician, Dr. Rodrigo Lopez, who had been accused of attempting to poison Queen Elizabeth."[17] Once he decided to write the play, he used the popular prejudices effectively in this play though considering Marlowe's presentation of the Jew, Shakespeare's may have gained a sympathetic nod from the present day theatre-goers.

However, the survival of the Shylock-stereotype on the stage is a proof of popular approval of these prejudices and their reluctance to reality-testing. Reflecting on the Shylock-stereotype Mary Mc Carthy clarified that Venetians in general were despised in the medieval period because they were all Shylocks. They were generally identified with Jews and to "the medieval mind, the Jew was the capitalist par excellence."[18] Jews were not allowed to own personal property and the ghetto was a Venetian invention where they were allowed to live in rented houses. They paid enormously to the Doge for their protection and survival and ultimately, as the historians tell us, both Venice and the Jews in Ghetto Nuovo became bankrupt. This pathetic survival of the Jews does not figure in *The Merchant of Venice.* Though Shylock pleads for it, he does not seem to be given a patient hearing and knowledgeable attention. The same aura of prejudicial strains becomes the cardinal feature for the remarkable survival of the stage-Jew over the centuries, with few conscientious portrayals by some kind Christian playwrights who presumably came in contact with the Jews. And yet conflicting attitudes began to surface against the Shylock that Shakespeare drew. The innumerable speculations reached a point where a critic wonders if it is possible to respond to the play as Shakespeare wanted, because there is a big gulf of time, and social attitudes have changed for better or for worse. Moody Prior gives an overview of the history of this play where he comments that different people view Shylock differently: some find him to be a tragic figure and some, a comic type. The advocates of Shylock as comic type justified the anti-Semitic overtone in the play, since a comedy has to rely on stock characters of society. Shylock criticism has three distinct classifications: historical, archetypal and thematic. Historical criticism probably goes back to the days of Venice and the Jewish life there, though Shakespeare discounts the fact that a commendable Rabbinical literature flourished during this period and Christian Venice is the major centre for Hebrew printing. The archetypal criticism rests on the argument that the Jew is the symbol of usury and the thematic studies are many and varied. After a vigorous discussion of the various interpretations over the years the critic comes to the conclusion that "Shylock haunts us because, in more senses than one, the world which he inhabits is unable to contain him."[19] And the story of the stage-life of Shylock continues.

In the long theatre history of the image of the Jew hardly any non-Jewish playwright bothered to risk a different, compassionate and realistic portrayal of the Jew though there are scattered examples here and there like Cumberland's *The Jew* (1894). Here, too, the dramatization of the Jew goes to the other extreme, conforming to the ingredients of another stereotype, this time it is the benevolent Jew—a complete contrast to the Shylock-stereotype. However, these benevolent stereotypes are few and far between. In either case the reality of the Jew disappears. Despite these figments of the imagination, there emerged a playwright, Lessing, whose play *Nathan the Wise* (1779) can be called the first major attempt from the non-Jews to create a Jew who bears resemblance to reality, though its success can be, once again, a matter of debate. These two examples bring forth a different perspective. While writing about the tradition of the stage-Jew, Ellen Schiff states that there is a marked difference in the treatment of the image of the Jew in the eighteenth century: "Beyond the mocking, mimicking and misrepresentation in the roles and images of Jews on the eighteenth and early nineteenth-century stage, one can dimly but unmistakably discern the silhouettes of genuine human beings. That is a giant step forward."[20] It is because of this change, some plays appeared with an altogether different view of the Jew. That there was such a change in the attitude is due to the blessings of the Age of Enlightenment which brought scepticism in the minds of the people. Religious prejudices slackened and so have the prejudices which resulted from dogmatic faith in the uniqueness of particular religions. Anti-Semitism which has a major source in religion—Jews supposedly crucified the Savior and rejected Him as a Messiah—grudgingly diminished. This seeming liberation gave the opportunity for the Jews to make an honest attempt at falling into the mainstream. Social intercourse, though it was initially embedded in problems, brought reality to the forefront which gave a different picture of the Jews to the conscientious Christians. *Nathan the Wise* is precisely a product of such a social intercourse between Gotthold Ephraim Lessing and the celebrated Judaic scholar, Moses Mendelssohn, who is the model for Nathan in the play. Mendelssohn was a strong believer in the Age of Enlightenment and was a source of inspiration and a guiding force for the Jewish *maskilim* who used all their efforts to take advantage of the newly available opportunities, at times going too far away from the tradition, and practising something which caused anxiety for the elderly patriarchs. Mendelssohn himself translated the Torah into German and consistently put in a major effort to bring about a certain interaction between German literature and culture and the Hebrew way of life. This tendency did not stop with him. Another famous philosopher, Herman Cohen, tried to establish a relationship between Immanuel Kant and Jewish philosophy. There were many such efforts which unquestionably looked rather radical to some people. Consequently, the Enlightenment, which in Jewish history is synonymous to the emancipation of the Jews from the Ghetto constraints, became the source of three important movements in the Jewish religion: Reform, Conservative, and neo-orthodoxy. Of all, Reform Judaism takes extensive inspiration from the ideas of Mendelssohn. It is this Mendelssohn, Lessing portrayed in *Nathan the Wise.* Being a believer in the emancipation of Jews, and their human rights, he preached tolerance and informed the prejudicial racial Germans that even Jews like Mendelssohn could be more benevolent than some of the Christians. The story of the Jewish Nathan who brings a Christian child up is a telling testimony to his humanity and unselfishness. Unlike the money-grubbing Shylock, he is generous and prepared to forego all the riches for the sake of the Christian child. The child never knows her origins for Nathan is not only a loving father but also a wise man who is the rock bed of human values. Though it hurts him, he has to conceal the past from the child's knowledge. In an American edition published in 1917, the editor quotes Kuno Fisher, whose essay on *Nathan the Wise* is, according to him, quite exhaustive. Fisher himself tries to give an interpretation which tries to see the milieu of a person as the responsible factor. Even in the Enlightenment, some notions of the naturalistic basis for man are obvious, which is again far from reality though no one can deny the social, political, economic and cultural restraining factors. Fisher's comments deserve to be quoted in full since he, once again, speculates a rationale for Shylock and Nathan on environmental level and doesn't question the authenticity of the stereotype of prejudice. Fisher, then, says:

> Take, now, a religion by nature intolerant and proud, the proudest, the most oppressed of all the religions in the world. Imagine a man permitted by his religion to esteem himself as the chosen of God, but condemned by the world, despised and rejected of men. If his soul yields to this two-fold pressure, and follows the natural course of human passions, it must be consumed by hatred and revenge. This must kindle a thirst for vengeance, so demoniacal, so beastly of flesh from an enemy's heart, if only to bait a hook with it. Yet, when these passions, which in their worst and lowest forms make a Shylock, are conquered by a noble soul—when tolerance is wrested from a religion at once the proudest and most oppressed, we have a Nathan.[21]

His argument is clear and it should be analyzed with the background of the Elizabethan social scene where there were no Jews officially, since they were expelled by King Edward. Their absence did not deter Shakespeare and there was no evidence that he practically indulged in reality-testing regarding their mean nature. And yet, instead of questioning the authenticity of such a portrayal, Fisher finds a rhetoric of justification though he allows that the Jews are the most oppressed people in the world. However, the negative prejudices do not influence him to the extent of writing a polemical essay on the play. It is worth considering some of the aspects of the play since Lessing also seems to have believed in the milieu theory that environmental conditioning is far greater and Shylocks can be the products of the suffocating Ghetto life of

Venice. The relevance of this will be discussed when we take up Wesker's *The Merchant.* Let us now turn to Lessing's play. Two aspects appear unmistakably in this play: one, Nathan as counter-Shylock; and two, the parable of the three rings preaching tolerance among major religions with the same source: Judaism, Christianity, and Islam. Nathan is aware of the usual racial prejudices directed against the Jews. When he is vexed with the pernicious assumption coming from Templar who saves his foster Christian child, he comments with inner rage:

despise my race
As much as e'er you please—we did not choose
Our races for ourselves. Do you and I
Make up our races?—What is a race forsooth—
Are Jews and Christians Christians and Jews
Rather than men? [22]

Universal humanism is only too evident in his words and this humanism as the message of all religions becomes a connecting thread in the parable of the three rings where three rings represent three religions. When this play was staged, there were mixed reactions. As is obvious from the rejoinders given by Lessing, there were many critics who felt that the image of the Jew was exaggerated, and far from reality. Lessing in his characteristic fashion gave a reply to the possibility of such a character as Nathan, provided there were better conditions. In one such rejoinder, he says: "My antagonist declares that such a Jew cannot be true to life, because he lives amid degradation and oppression and is obliged to subsist solely by trade. Granted, but does not it necessarily follow that the improbability is not eliminated if these adverse circumstances are changed? But when can this come to pass? Undoubtedly, only when the Jew begins to feel the scorn and obloquy of the Christians in a lesser degree and is not constrained to eke out a wretched existence in petty, despicable barter. What then becomes the next requisite? Affluence? O Yes, the right use of riches is also of prime importance."[23] True enough, Nathan is a rich man and is a man of good nature. Though it is an extreme argument to conclude that the Jews who live in ghettoes are necessarily Shylocks, there is a shift in the focus of the argument. Whereas Shylock in Shakespeare's play is a Jewish money-grubber with all the attributes of an anti-Christ, Lessing's view changes the significance of this perspective. He seems to remark that if Shylock is sub-human and venal, it is not because of his religion, but because of the environment and degrading circumstances. This takes away the religious stigma from his life and it gives him a status of an individual, like any other person, who can be vulnerable. And like any other person, he also can be benevolent or surreptitious, depending on his environment and the external social aspects. This view is the essential blessing of the spirit of Englightenment which gave an opportunity for many Jews to participate in the mainstream of the country and, whenever given an opportunity, he made an indelible impact on the development of ideas in art, culture and politics.

Despite certain blessings of the Englightenment, it also sparked off controversies with regard to Jewish loyalty and patriotism. This is not without its own rationalism. Jewish life in Diaspora is essentially nationalistic. Their rituals, festivals and even their language, Yiddish or Ladino, is symbolic of Jewish nationalism which fervently hopes to return to the Promised Land. Consequently, it gave a false impression to the people that Jews form a state within a state. In fact, Napoleon also was forced to seek opinions regarding this issue though he provided legal and civil rights to the French Jews in his time. When citizenship was granted to the Jews, they made the provision with caution: ''Indicative of the disparity between principle and personal attitudes toward the Jews was the emphasis made in the Assembly's deliberations on the obvious fact that the rights of the citizens granted to the Jews appertain to the Jew *qua* individual and not the Jew *qua* nation. Presumably, it is the Jew *qua* member of the Jewish nation who bears all the egregious qualities that evoke the French-man's fears.''[24]

However, it did not take much time for anti-Semitic prejudices to reemerge. The Dreyfuss Affair in France, the persecution of

Yiddish writers and the other Jews in the Post-October Revolution Russia, and the influence of rhetoric of prejudice in Richard Wanger and his compatriots's writings hold an eloquent testimony to this fact. This came as a severe blow to the Jewish writer. No reader of Isaac Babel, Sholom Aleichem, David Bergelson and many Yiddish writers in Russia, can forget the burden of anxiety effectively suggested in their poetry, fiction and drama. Commenting on the persecution of the Jews, Khone Shmeruk states that one "wishes to find some crumb of logic even among these fantastic and heavy handed crimes. There is no doubt that an important role was played by the deep-rooted anti-Semitism which received during and after the war."[25]

The prejudices always have sources, myths, stereotypes to fall back on. The myth of the Wandering Jew, the Shylock-stereotype, and the usual pretexts for anti-Semitism become a regular subject for the invective. Stefen Heym, who is a wanderer himself, wrote *The Wandering Jew* (1984), which deals with this myth satirically. Since this myth is also an extension of stereotypes of prejudice, it cannot be ignored in the discussion. In this novel, he explores the genesis of the myth, sometimes with the allegorical strain of the contemporary social scene. Writing about the myth of the wandering Jew, George Anderson says that all the major religions have examples of legends of an Eternal Wanderer: "The wandering Jew, Cain, Al-Sameri, Pindola, the Wild Huntsman, the Flying Dutchman, and the peculiar Armenian contribution, Peter Rugt all blasphemed, or were at least disobedient to God."[26] Anderson does not try to discuss the validity and reality of the wandering Jew. However, Heym's book is a record of centuries of religious bigotry perpetrated against the Jews. At the same time, he does not belittle or ignore the religious inspiration of Christ. Between the long theological arguments, the stark reality of persecution is revealed. Beyond the continuing satire, as Ernst Pawel believes, there is anxiety because "after the centuries of violence in the name of perennial myths, it only requires unquestioned faith to believe that mankind can survive the weapons of mass destruction."[27] Originally this myth of wandering Jew started with a popularly conceived tale that at the time of Crucifixion Ahasuerus refused to give water to the thirsty Christ. Christ curses him to walk the earth till his second coming. Even this myth is challenged by Franz Werfel, a German dramatist, whose play was adopted by S.N. Behrman entitled *Jacobowsky and the Colonel* (1944) where Behrman presents a cheerful, human and sacrificing Wandering Jew who is eager to flee the Germans. Though his companion the colonel is an anti-Semite, Jacobowsky proves his humanity by sacrificing what is dear to him even in the most trying circumstances of survival. This discussion proves that though the much talked about Jewish emancipation was a blessing in a way, it could never wipe out the deep-rooted prejudices. The fact that there are many negative Jewish images in the nineteenth-century English fiction confirms this assumption. Celebrated novelists like Charles Dickens, Daphne du Maurier, Mary Shelly and George Eliot presented Jews in their novels. Though the latter novelist's treatment is not unsympathetic the rest of the novelists still stick to the traditional stereotypes with little or no modifications. Throughout these centuries where the negative stereotypes flooded Christian civilization, there were Hebrew and Yiddish literatures which presented the authentic Jewish problems as many anthologies sufficiently testify. For instance, in the same nineteenth-century England, some Jewish writers—Israel Zangwill, the most important of all—took the responsibility of fighting the negative Jewish types in their works but their readership was not as widespread as that of their other English counterparts.

The persistent anti-Semitism which is the source of the stereotypes worried even the most enlightened and assimilated, as it did in the case of Theodor Herzl whose fervent Zionism became the sustaining force that finally led to the formation of Israel. Having witnessed the trial in the Dreyfuss Affair, he realized how difficult and immediate the problem of anti-Semitism was. From then on, he spent the rest of his life in putting his intellectual resources together to solve this problem forever. The only way to solve this problem would be to have a different place for Jews. However, Zionism as a concept has many ramifications: political, cultural, theological, and literary. In Wesker's play, having lost everything to the obnoxious prejudices of the gentiles, Shylock Kolner decides to go to Jerusalem—the Promised Land of the Jews. That is the only possible solution he could think of. Herzl, along with many more Zionists like Yehuda Halevi, became a beacon light for this new awareness. Hitler's persecution and the Holocaust only hastened the process. Having discussed these movements and issues and conceptual classifications, we can now discuss Wesker's *The Merchant*. The discussion of this play is delayed because one has to be aware of the things that had happened before, since either directly or indirectly most of these events echo in this play. Also, Wesker wrote this play after extensive research. He was conscious of many cultural, political, and theological aspects of the events that took place and the relevance they have to Jewish history. More importantly, there is an urgent need to present the case as it is and bring it out into the open and face up to it so that a liberation from the centuries of abstraction is at last possible. Hence, one finds so many surprises and contrasts from the original Shakespeare play.

In Wesker's version, Shylock and Antonio are not rivals but intimate friends in their mid-sixties. Their different religions and the restraining Venetian laws do not discourage their friendship. Shylock is not merely a money-lender but is a perspicacious bibliophile and a scholar in Hebrew theology and scholarship. Ghetto Nuovo is not the breeding place for human hatred but a place alive with Jewish scholars coming from various countries to spend their time in scholarly company with Shylock and the other co-religionists. Jessica does not reject her father in favour of Christian company and Christian grace and redemption. But she stands her ground to defend her father and scorn at the manipulation of the Venetian laws and their blatant inhumanity. The bond is not a vengeful one but it is a mockery of their laws, particularly meant for the Jews of Venice. One also finds a more realistic dramatization of Shtetl-life.

The play opens with Shylock and Antonio—old friends busy with bibliographical arrangements of ancient Hebrew books Shylock painstakingly, and at the risk of his life, had collected, for the

Talmud and many other Jewish books were banned. One can see flashes of Jewish humour in their banter. Having been cheered up with wine, Antonio asks Shylock if he is religious at all. Shylock is a freethinker with his rationalistic attitude towards his religion. He says it is like pimples in adolescence, and he cannot escape being religious. But Antonio is not a religious man. Shylock asks Antonio to stay at his home, though it is forbidden to do so for a Christian. Shylock tells him that he can take care of the consequences for he knows that a little bribe can make the authorities overlook anything. Act One has six scenes and in these six scenes the audience gets an opportunity to look at various aspects of Jewish life. One can perceive the friendship between Shylock and Antonio; Jessica's refusal to be controlled by her father and his ideas and her belief that her father is an intellectual snob; the persecuted Jews from Portugal temporarily seeking refuge in Ghetto Nuovo; the affection between Shylock and his sister Rivka forever showing generosity and hospitality; Bassanio's need forcing Antonio to take money from Shylock on a mock-bond since no Christian can enter into a deal with a Jew unless there is a bond; the intellectual side of Shylock's family honouring celebrated Jewish scholars, painters; and the preconceived notions of the Gentiles against the Jew though they hardly meet them in their lives. These scenes are effectively written to give not a stereotypical view one generally finds in the stage history of the Jews, but an authentic side of Jewish life. At the same time, Wesker does not digress from the main theme of the play. In these scenes one finds Jewish humour, parental crisis, the anxiety of wandering Jews owing to persecution and the day-to-day problems of paying enormous taxes so that the Jews in Venice can live with state protection. The tension in Shylock's family, threats from outside, concern for the fellow-Jews's plight and communal activities do not take the essential humanity away from Shylock. In fact, they make him more human and alive to the facts of the situations. For the state's protection, the Jews have to pay enormous sums to the government and contribute to the local Churches. The social life of the Jews is intolerable. Ghettoes are overpacked and susceptible to frequent fire accidents. They are not hygienic and hardly any light comes into the ghetto houses. Despite all these miseries, there are frequent pressures from the state, demanding more money. And, of course, the usual prejudices of the gentiles towards them is harrowing. This is evident in Bassanio's remarks. He thinks there are thousands of Jews in Venice when, in reality, they are only fourteen hundred. He never met a Jew and still he is negatively preoccupied with them. He seems to have taken everything his society gave him by way of negative attitudes and prejudices. He is largely influenced by the socially preconceived notions. Consequently, when there is a possibility of reality-testing of his views, he is taken aback by the unbridgeable gulf. Graziano's information regarding Jews startles him. On the other hand, Lorenzo also seems to have fed on the prejudicial social stereotypes when he says about Jessica: "You'd not think they are of the same blood. He's proud, she's modest. He imagines knowledge is all, she lives in the world. His voice is metallic with contempt, hers is sweet with reason. And she listens to music."[28] Although this description can by no means be called prejudiced, Lorenzo is still influenced by the traditional attitudes. Traditionally, the Jewess is a benevolent figure unlike the cannibalistic Jew. Lorenzo falls back on this myth. However, Lorenzo is sensitive and is capable of preventing non-conformist ideas like his distaste for merchandizing and authorities from influencing him in his judgements.

Wesker also pays attention to the political authorities of the Doge and the history of usury and how, since Christians cannot practise it, it is thrust upon the Jew. Having done that, they have a permanent pretext to criticize the money-grabbing attitude of the Jew. Jews, on their part, are not allowed to own personal property, and no professions are open for them. Crammed into the ghettoes, usury is the only profession they could practise. Helpless, aware of the external menace and the utility of money for their protection, they are forced to stick to it, thus living the role thrust upon them by the Christians. In the first act of the play, Shylock appears concerned about the plight of his nation. Schooled in the practical wisdom of centuries, he knows his priorities. And yet his friendship with Antonio and his interest in scholarship, learning and cultural activities does not wane to any lesser degree. One sees many instances to this effect in the play. However, Shylock is not intelligible to Bassanio, Graziano and Lorenzo when he finally meets them. He retells the history of Venice and Rome to the people and its three distinct developments. His knowledge surprises them when he says there was a synagogue much before the Papacy in Rome. These three developments are told only to conclude symbolically that the inhumanity that is perpetrated on the Jew underscores all these developments. The printed books speak volumes for an objective onlooker. He appreciates the painstaking efforts of Cassiodorus for preserving even the pagan collections. The same person said: "We cannot enforce acceptances of a creed, since no one can be compelled to believe against his will."[29] This is a tolerant view but the fact remains that there were Roman wars and Jewish slaves. Phase one is completed with the death of Cassiodorus in A.D. 575. Thus the glorious day of Rome is completed. In phase two, the Roman Empire is destroyed and Italy breaks into three pieces. The introduction of city-states meant government. With the rise of industry and trades, they invented "partnership agreement, holding companies, marine insurance, credit transfers, double-entry book-keeping."[30] But they got the ideas from the books preserved by Cassiodorus. The third development is Gutenburg printing which immediately made the classical writers known to every body. When he concludes this narration, the bell rings and soon the ghetto is to be closed. Shylock must go. He takes his yellow-hat and "goes off chuckling and mumbling." (44) The audience gets the impression of this enormous vista of progress and wonders as to where the Jew figures and why he is excluded from their progress. The answers for the tolerant Christians are immediately available. Antonio is one such Christian.

And that is the reason why he insists that there should be a legal bond and not the "nonsense-bond" of a pound of flesh. But Shylock's humanity and rage against the law that defines him and his nation reacts to it and, for once, he has an opportunity to mock at it and prove how subhuman these laws are. Here, Shylock does not foresee the consequences. But Antonio, being a patrician, knows only too well. He tries to convince him:

> You are a Jew, Shylock. Not only is your race a minority, it is despised. Your existence here in Venice, your leisures, your very freedom to be sardonic or bitter is a privilege, not a right. Your life, the lives of your people depend upon contract and your respect for the laws behind contract, just as your contract with the city councillor *they* must respect. Therefore you, of all people, have need of the respect for the law. The law, Shylock, the law! For you and your people, the bond-in-law must be honoured.[31]

Finally, there is the legal bond of a strange nature. Antonio is to give a "pound of flesh" if the money is not paid within a stipulated time—Shylock mocking the law that mocks his people! The second act of the play presents new characters: Portia and Nerissa. And there are serious problems to trouble Shylock. His daughter runs away from home, disaster for Antonio, for his ships are sunk, and more disaster for Shylock because of the complexity of the bond which can be interpreted as a conspiracy against the Venetian citizen, which may cause serious damage to his life, his wealth and his fellow men. Disaster does occur to Shylock but not before the full disclosure of the vanity of laws. Jessica's refusal to be coaxed into Christianity and her defence of her father and the ultimate rejection of the Christian lover is suggestive of the demythification of the age-old stereotype of the good Jewess who by finally converting herself to Christianity becomes a telling message that a Jew is irredeemably anti-Christian, voluptuous, cannibalistic and devilish whereas the Jewess is graceful, for she accepts the faith in Jesus. It does not take much time for her to realize that, after all, she has made a wrong choice. Her consistent protest against their vile charges against her father, religion, and their ignorance of Jewish life in the ghettoes give a different picture than that of the all too familiar Shakespearean stereotype.

In the court scene, conventional charges are levelled against Shylock. Antonio furiously rejects the conde[illegible]ation of Jewish usury. He states that the Jew is forced to pursue what he detests and by doing that he is relieving the sin from the Christians. He continues: ''Do we condemn the Jew for doing what our system has required him to do? Then if we do, let's swear, upon the cross, that among us we know of no Christian, no patrician, no duke, bishop or merchant who in his secret chambers, does not lend at interest, for that's what usury is.''[32] As this discussion is in progress, Graziano remarks that the Jew is ungrateful. Then Shylock recounts the historical fabrications that are thrust upon the Jew so that the political systems, authorities, and institutions can survive by avoiding the main issue by cleverly diverting the public attention on to the archetypal scapegoat. Shylock talks explicitly of the centuries of outrage: ''Your wars go wrong, the Jew must be the cause of it; your economic systems crumble there the Jew must be; your wives get sick of you—a Jew will be an easy target. Failed university, professional blundering, self-loathing—the Jew, the Jew, the cause, the Jew. And when will you cease?''[33] Though the crisis of the bond is solved by ingenious Portia, Shylock forgoes his wealth. And he finally gets ready to go to Jerusalem and a woman's sad Sephardic song is heard from the background—a song of ancestral journey on the fringes of society, bearing witness to man's inhumanity towards man.

His life is at last redeemed from the assumptions that fix him to a stereotype. He emerges as an individual who is judged by others for his religion and social role in an unfavourable way, not because he deserves it but because he is thrown into the trap of age-old prejudices. The portrayal of Wesker's Shylock liberates him and puts him on a different perspective, ultimately demythifying the stereotype.

Ludwig Lewisohn's Shylock in *The Last Days of Shylock* (1931) also attempts to depict the agony of Shylock. Beginning with the post-trial experience, this novel sympathetically communicates the life-story of Shylock who, as typical of any Jew in those times, has sad memories of the mass killings of Jews, oppression and humiliations at the hands of the Christian. The novel tries to communicate the historical background which makes Shylock's predicament more poignant. Although it begins where the Shakespearean play ends, the author takes the opportunity to view the past of Shylock in order to provide a useful social history. Unlike Shakespeare's Jessica who elopes with Lorenzo, Jessica of this novel meets her father in Eretz Yisroel where her father, wounded and exhausted, comes to spend his last years. They quickly make peace and Shylock spends the rest of his life with his grandchildren. Shylock comes out of the stereotypical structure and emerges as a person who suffered a raw deal at the hands of the Christians but finally finds consolation in the Zionist idea. The novel understandably received appreciation from the Jewish community leaders like Rabbi Finkelstein, Rabbi Stephen Wise and, the great Jewish scholar and translator, Maurice Samuel.

Western civilization which ostensibly expounded theories of humanism paradoxically meted out arbitrary justice to the Jew and by indulging in such a lapse put humanism on trial, for, humanist philosophy couldn't afford to bypass the inhuman treatment of the Jew. The fact that the Jew survived this ordeal speaks of his affirmation of humanity. Applying the causes of the prejudices, as is discussed at the beginning of this overview, one clearly perceives the reasons for the sustenance of official and religious anti-Semitism. This elaborate overview brings to an end the general Jewish history with its tumultuous chapters of pogroms, massacres and occasional respite which no contemporary Jewish writer forgets.

With these views in mind, it will be interesting to study American Jewish drama and the thematic concerns of Jewish playwrights. Though the same old stereotypes appeared on the American stage of the eighteenth and the nineteenth centuries, some early Jewish playwrights like David Belasco avoided altogether the Jewish themes and Jewish characters in their plays although David Belasco presents a Jew in a play called *Men and Women* (1890). But here too he is too eager to present a benevolent Jew—another extreme stereotype. Israel Cohen in this play falls in love with a gentile girl who is also loved by another person. The usual intricacies of the triangle story get resolved after a series of surprises and entanglements. In the process, Israel Cohen emerges as a

Sheva-stereotype, too good to be true. In more than a hundred plays he wrote in collaboration with others, this is probably the only play in which he discusses the Jewish problem which is, to say the least, surprising. Louis Harap[34] in his outstanding work focusses on the controversy the Shylock stereotype created among the Jews. At the turn of the century, the American Jews are fairly well-established and their community organizations are active enough to take up the challenge of negative criticism. With the immigrants flooding America, the Jew with the Yiddish accent and broken English became a stock comic figure in American drama of the nineteenth century. The Jewish journals protested against this practice. Against this background, David Belasco's play should be assessed. He avoided Jewish themes and Jewish characters in the play because if he had to introduce them, he could only introduce them as individuals, since he was a Jew himself. Small wonder Israel Cohen is such a benevolent and all-sacrificing person.

Royall Tyler—the first American dramatist to write a play called *The Contrast* which is truly American in its subject matter and manner—also wrote some plays on biblical episodes. Nevertheless, he does not seem to be successful in extricating himself from the influence of the times. In his plays on Purim, which is depicted in the book of Esther being the story of Haman's conspiracy to wipe out the Jewish community with a mind on political power, Tyler reflects the conventional rhetoric against the Jews, though this time, it comes from the characters like Haman who blissfully calls Mordecai a reptile Jew, vile Jew and a beast. Further, Tyler gives a Christian slant to the biblical episode. His comments sometimes appear to be influenced by contemporary prejudices:

> O vile disgrace!
> Troops of their hated race, crowded the streets
> And shook their greasy Jewish gaberdines
> And seem'd in mockery to say, "Who now
> Doth bow."[35]

Tyler seems to be making vile comments against the newly arrived immigrants in America. Otherwise, he does not seem to be familiar with Jewish rituals. It is possible to say that he is simply interested in giving vent to his usual Christian interpretation of the scriptures of the Jewish contexts. Hence he talks about the prophecy being fulfilled by the Saviour of mankind. Esther, not surprisingly, kneels and prays. When ultimately the crisis is resolved a chorus of Jews celebrates "the God of our Salvation." Apart from the Christian slant to a Jewish episode, the author can find justification for the derogatory comments against the Jews on the only pretext that these words are spoken by Haman who is a Jew-hater himself and so it fits into the situation. Compared to the play we have mentioned, *Joseph and His Brethren* seems to be more faithful to the original since there is no extensive Christian references and, in fact, Judah speaks Hebrew. However, Tyler takes the opportunity to give an evangelical message to reform his fellow-Christians in *The Wisdom of Solomon*. Although he tells the proverbial story of Solomon's wisdom when he is to solve the problem of finding out who the real mother is, he also preaches true Christianity of "the gospel sun" in order to "gain the honour of the Christian name." For this purpose both prologue and epilogue are effectively used. It will be an exaggeration to infer from these biblical plays a streak of the author's anti-Semitism. At the same time, it is an equally difficult proposition to reach a conclusion that Tyler is tolerant towards the Jews. What can be safely deduced from these plays is that, he at least does not deny the unquestionable relationship between Judaism and Christianity. One could even argue that it is subversive from the Jewish viewpoint, to use what is obviously a Jewish context to preach the Christian gospel. It can also be said that the very fact that he is using these Jewish episodes for Christian purposes—in fact, it is minimal in the last two plays—can be tolerantly viewed as an attempt at mutual acceptance at a time when so many immigrants were living in America. Which, incidentally, should not make one overlook the fact that even the first American playwright, who vowed to write American plays with no bias or influence of the European literary or cultural ethos, could not be free from Jewish stereotypes.

These stereotypes continued to haunt the American stage in the twentieth century though they are met with tremendous disapproval. The decisive break however came not with the gentile tolerance but with the emrgence of the Jewish writer in the twenties and the thirties *from* the self-conscious talebearer with the patronage of Jewish readership *to* the preeminent position of a major voice in America. His creative endeavour commented on and reflected the secular themes along with Jewish themes, or when it is entirely secular, interpreted it with an undeniable Jewish sensibility. The story of the American Jewish writer from the position of writing for the Jewish readership—Henry Roth, Daniel Fuchs, Edward Dahlberg, Meyer Levin figure in this category, to name only a few—to the *mainstream* voice has contributed a great deal to the final death blow to the stereotype. The very fact that they are writing in English, not in Hebrew or Yiddish, suggests their acceptance by or at least the readership of, the WASP culture, not to mention the role played by Jewish assimilation.

However, this gave rise to other kinds of stereotypes, this time fostered and nourished by Jewish writers themselves. The practical and protective Jewish mother who is caricatured ruthlessly, and certainly with unjustifiable outrage, in Philip Roth's *Porthoy's Complaint* and the devout, unworldly and innocent father have occupied the disguise of stereotypes in certain works. But they are harmless acts of self-criticism which is an integral part of Jewish humour and Jewish sensibility. Liberated to a large extent from the burden of stereotypical notions, the Jewish writer ventured to visualize not only the predicament of being a Jew in troubled times of contemporary decadence but also judged the inhumanity of the world with a prophetic rage. Jewish hunger and concern for social justice and ethical culture that can accommodate the bereaved soul of modern man, to speak in universal terms, largely moved the imagination of Jewish writers. The outcome of such ventures and trials both in terms of aesthetic achievement and in terms of social, political and cultural ambience will be assessed in the following pages.

NOTES

1. Paul Edward, ed., *Encyclopedia Britannica,* Vol. 11 (London: William Benton, 1929, 1961), p. 876.
2. *The Encyclopedia of Philosophy,* Vol. 4 (New York: The Macmillan, 1967), pp. 69-70.
3. *Ibid.*, p. 72.
4. J.P. Van Praag, "What is Humanism?," *The Humanist Alternative: Some Definitions of Humanism,* ed. Paul Kurtz (New York: Prometheus Books, 1973), p. 43.
5. H.J. Blackham, "A Definition of Humanism," *The Humanist Alternative*, p. 37.
6. David L. Sills, ed., *International Encyclopedia of the Social Sciences* (New York: The Macmillan and Free Press, 1968), p. 259.
7. Walter Lippmann, *Public Opinion* (New York: Free Press, 1922), p. 53.
8. *Ibid.*, p. 59.
9. John Harding, *International Encyclopedia of the Social Sciences,* p. 259.
10. T.W. Adorno et al, *The Authoritarian Personality* (New York: Harper and Row, 1950), p. 57.
11. Bruno Bettelheim, *Social Change and Prejudice* (New York: Free Press, 1950), p. 136.
12. Arnold Wesker, *The Merchant* (London: Methuen, 1977), p. XLIX.
13. *Ibid.*
14. *Ibid.*, p. LIV.
15. Joshua Trachtenberg, *The Devil and the Jew* (New York: Meridian, 1943).
16. Jacob Marcus, ed., *The Jew in the Medieval World* (New York: A Temple Book, 1983).
17. *Ibid.*, p. 367. In fact, the "pound of flesh" theme appeared in Gregorio Leti's *Vita di Sisto V* which, as Marcus surmises, appeared a century after the publication of Shakespeare's play in which the victim is a Jew and villain is a Christian. This, however, is supposed to have taken place in 1587 though scholars are not inclined to accept its authenticity.
18. Mary Mc Carthy, *Venice Observed.* (London: Heinemann, 1956, 1961), p. 36.

19. Moody E. Prior, "Which is the Jew that Shakespeare Drew?," *The American Scholar* (Autumn, 1981).
20. Ellen Schiff, *From Stereotype to Metaphor* (Albany: State University of New York Press, 1982), p. 19.
21. Kuno Fisher, quoted in the Kohut's introduction to Lessing's *Nathan the Wise* (New York: Black Publishing Company, 1917), p. 29.
22. Gotthold Ephrain Lessing, *Nathan the Wise*, p. 210.
23. Lessing quoted in Kohut's introduction to *Nathan the Wise*, p. 39.
24. Mendes-Flohr, R. Paul and Jehuda Reinharz, ed., *The Jew in the Modern World* (New York: Oxford University Press, 1980), p. 101.
25. Irving Howe and Eliezer Greenberg, ed., *Ashes Out of Hope* (New York: Schocken Books, 1977), p. 20.
26. George Anderson, *The Legend of the Wandering Jew* (Providence: Brown University, 1965), p. 3.
27. Ernst Pawel, *New York Times Book Review* (Feb. 20, 1984), p. 14.
28. Arnold Wesker, *The Merchant* (London: Methuen, 1977), p. 28.
29. *Ibid.*, p. 41.
30. *Ibid.*, p. 43.
31. *Ibid.*, p. 25.
32. *Ibid.*, p. 75.
33. *Ibid.*, p. 77.
34. Louis Harap, *The Image of the Jew in American Literature* (Philadelphia: The Jewish Publication Society of America, 1974). The author, in his chapter on the nineteenth century treatment of the Jew, gives a detailed survey of the negative stereotypes on the American stage which eventually, caused many Jewish organizations and Jewish journals to take a stronger view against such prejudices. David Belasco was obviously aware of all these controversies and hence, understandably, avoided Jewish figures in his plays, though Jewish humanism towards the little man in society has been a major theme in some of his plays.
35. Royall Tyler, *The Origin of the Feast of Purim in America's Lost Plays* (Bloomington: Indiana University Press, 1940, 1965), p. 55.
36. *Ibid.*, p. 62.
37. Royall Tyler, *The Wisdom of Solomon* in *The America's Lost Plays*, p. 120.

America Gonef: The American Dream and the Jewish Dilemma

> Before coming to America he (the writer's father) had been a Jewish peasant in the Ukraine. He had run a mill, as well. A man of the land, he was to spend most of his life in sweat shops after he arrived, in 1895, at the age of thirty five. And he was never to know anything good no matter where he worked in New York. For it was the wrong time for a man of half skills who preferred God to the making of money to be in the United States of America. My mother, who was not financially illiterate, was soon calling America "America, Gonef."[1]

Harry Roskolenko, a Jewish writer, is speaking for many Jewish immigrant families when he asserts that the Jewish life at the turn of the century and the early part of the 20th century has been a span of horrendous days. The Jews who came to America with golden dreams from the Old Country soon realized that they have so much to suffer to make a decent living. Meat shops and garment industries took a heavy toll of their lives. Little wonder they became disillusioned for, as Oscar Handlin rightly puts it in his sociological study entitled *The Uprooted,* the immigrant life is burdened with a sense of alienation and miserable consequences. It does not mean that they became pessimistic but the gulf between the American dream and social reality is something that they could not envisage. Hence there are quick reactions to the American dream which can be found in the works of Mary Antin, Abraham Cahan, Budd Schulberg, Henry Roth, Edward Dahlberg, Nathaniel West and many more to follow later as the decades wore on. Not all works are, however, skeptical and at least, Mary Antin's *The Promised Land* (1912), subtly celebrates America just as Emma Lazarus's poem on the Statue of Liberty talks about the liberation of the "Huddled Masses" because of the possibilities in America. Even in the most engaging portrayals of irony implied in the American dream, there are always some people who seem to have been haunted by it, who accept the dubious terms that become part of the realization of the dream which finally alienates themselves from the saner side of life. This may finally take him to the extreme point of death because of the conflicting dilemma in themselves after having accepted the ethics of the dream. However, other characters in the same work, either a play or a novel or a poem, remain tuned with the rhythm of society. Even so, he cannot bring himself to the position of either whole-heartedly accepting the available means or practising the dictates of the inhuman ways to realize the dream.

This ambivalent attitude can be perceived in many of the Jewish writers throughout almost a century of Jewish American literature. The two most important works in this direction are Mary Antin's *The Promised Land* and Abraham Cahan's *The Rise of David Levinsky* (1917), both spell out two different themes which later are to become consistently associated with Jewish writers in America. In Mary Antin's version there is a celebration of the American dream, fully endorsing assimilation, and in fact claiming that it is her second birth. While giving a picture of the Russian Jewish life she welcomes the blessings of American freedom. Throughout her autobiography, one never finds any apologies or regrets. She writes about the process from the Russian ghettoes to the Lower East Side tenements: "All the processes of uprooting, transportation, replanting acclimatization, and development took place in my own soul. I feel the pang, the fear, the wonder, and the joy of it."[2] Though she wants to forget the past and is concerned with the present, she never ignores the past. While one cannot read a perspective stating that she accommodates both the past and the present, there is also reason to believe that she is perfectly in touch with the American scene. Cahan's David Levinsky is a different example. His problem is that he does not know how to accommodate the past with the present. Instead, he constantly wanders between the extremes of sentimentalizing on "making it" in America. He makes it to the top of the success ladder only to feel the misery of alienation, guilt and spiritual exhaustion. A *yeshiva* boy himself in Russia, he comes to America and becomes a millionaire businessman, with all the anxieties and cruel competitive techniques that make him successful. At the end of this long novel—which is not a true autobiography like Mary Antin's but a fictionalized autobiography of Levinsky who is a prototype of the immigrant Jew—Levinsky is left with his riches, a sense of loss, and a haunting need for the redeeming past: "I can never forget the days of my misery. I cannot escape from my old self. My past and my present do not compose well. David, the poor lad swinging over a Talmud volume at the Preacher's Synogogue, seems to have more in common with my inner identity than David Levinsky, the well known cloak manufacturer."[3]

Though the Jewish playwrights of contemporary America did not exclusively deal with the Jews or presented Jews in their plays specifically, their attitudes towards the American dream remained ambivalent in many ways. Starting from Ludwig Lewisohn's *Adam* to the recent David Mamet's *American Buffalo,* there appears a streak of skepticism, sometimes an effective demythification of the revered dream of upward mobility and the price one has to pay for it. It would be interesting to analyze some of these plays where the ambivalent view figures prominently. For this purpose four approaches are selected and to substantiate them suitable plays are taken up for discussion. In the first approach, Ludwig Lewisohn's *Adam* is discussed to suggest that the Jewish self-hatred is the psychological factor which takes them away from anything Jewish which unwittingly prepares the way for self-entrapment or identity crisis. Since this play is written at a time when Jewish assimilationism in America was intense, it becomes all the more authentic in this connection. It is also one of the few plays that outline the Zionist idea as a resolution to perpetual anti-Semitism. In the second approach Murray Schisgal's *Pushcart Peddlers* and Israel

Horowitz's *The Indian Wants the Bronx* are chosen which depict immigrant hopes. The third approach concentrates on Jewish communal life in America and the changes that are taking place. This part of the discussion mainly centres round religion, customs and other Jewish patterns with selected plays from Paddy Chayefsky and others. The fourth approach takes up the myth of the American dream and its allurements. Clifford Odets, David Mamet and Arthur Miller figure in this section. Even popular fiction is filled with the irony of the American dream. In the novels of Howard Fast, Cynthia Freeman, Herbert Gold—to name only a few—one finds a constant negation of the dream.

However, instead of simply presenting the social reality and the American ideals, Lewisohn tries to explore the reasons for the willing assimilations of Adam Elhar and the reasons for his suicide since he sadly realizes that he is not successful in assimilating himself to a gentle society and be accepted by it. It is a play where the main character never appears on stage. The whole argument and details centre round his life, his success and his death, it is Lewisohn's superb dramaturgy that keeps the audience attention stuck to the central theme and never, for a moment, strays from it. The play has a prologue and an epilogue and in between there are seven scenes which tell the life and death of Adam Elhar. But the play has many thematic levels. For a one-play author, Lewisohn has shown an enormous sense of theatre.

The prologue takes up to Roman times. Israel was under Roman rule after the destruction of the Temple. The three rabbis withdraw themselves to a safe place. After long deliberation, Rabbi Akiba Ben Joseph decides to fight the Romans with arms which looks impractical to Rabbi Ismael Ben Elisha and Rabbi Tarphon. They find justification in the Hebrew scriptures in their no-war plea but Akiba cannot be deterred. A true Jew and a man of his community whose word is valued, he comes from a farming class. He resents the interaction between Greeks and Hebrews, which he fears would finally destroy the chosenness or exclusiveness. He says: "Our people will obey God, not Aristotle."[4] Forced to respond to the assumption that it may be possible in the distant future that the

Greek influence will be overwhelming, Akiba says that Israel must follow what he says and practice the teachings of the Torah. Consequently even when the Greek influence becomes predominant, it cannot change their character for "they will have become so unalterably themselves—they and the Torah will be so utterly one, that each will live the Torah even though he knows it not and that the very apostate in his apostasy will practice the law." (8) If this apostasy proves too uncontrollable, Akiba predicts, he will die of it. Adam's life becomes a testimony to prove this thesis.

In the succeeding seven scenes, Adam's tryst with the entire gentile society and the reluctance of the latter to accept him due to the traditional prejudice and the reaction of various people towards him, convincingly portray his tortuous ambitions and the underlying pathos. In these scenes, different people show various versions of prejudice. In the first scene, the two English people state that Adam does not appear to be English, his origins are obscure and his name is peculiar. Yet the English gentleman admits that he is decent in obliging him when he had recommended someone for a job. Jackie who is offered the job doesn't really appreciate it, because they are "new people" and it is "dreadful" to work with them. In the second scene, Lucy Elhar is back to her parent's home because she finds it difficult to stay with him. He appears slovenly at parties, participating only for the sake of ritual, and she thinks he is "freezing up" in his heart. He does not like to have a child because there would be no place for it in this hostile world. And still, Lucy admits that he is a good Christian. The latter part of the play is to prove that he is a Jew and lives an anonymous life. True enough her brother informs her that he is a Jew. What is significant here is that her mother consistently supports him. Next scene shifts to Elhar's office in New York. Here again the gentile attitude is painful to him. When the clerk is dismissed she says that she is not interested in working with Jews and Jewish companies. She blames her inadequacies on the supposed taking over of America by the Jews. Now she is determined to work with only a Christian company. In the same scene the Jewish manager is worried because his wife is obsessed with her Christian friends and her behaviour makes his children loathe being Jewish. The third aspect of the scene emerges when the stenographer also decides to quit since she heard so much about the Elders of Zion—a book published in France which states that the Jews all over the world have a conspiracy to take over the entire world. In these scenes, one can see the development of the central theme. The fourth scene is about Adam's love, who decides to go with her friend to Germany. Her friend on the other hand has a prejudicial attitude towards him with the conventional notions which make him identify Adam with the mythical wandering Jew who is cursed and smudges "every bright surface they touch." (56) The fifth scene is crucial because here three Jews try to reason out on some issues related to Adam. The first Jew assesses Adam's life in terms of self-hatred. He knows that Adam is trying to prove to the world that a Jew can be just as good as others. He is a wealthy man now liberally donating to humanitarian causes only to expiate his guilt. And yet he is not one with the world because in "his bones are still the ghetto fears. He is still amazed and dazzled by being out in the world. His subconscious still beats him by that privilege over and over again by showing how good an American, how broad minded humanitarian a Jew can be." (63) To prove this, he is to flee from his own self and his Jewish past. And there must be a serious reason for his escape from Jewish consciousness. In this tension-ridden atmosphere, Lewisohn presents Adam's parents: the pious Jewish family. His father Eliasberg, a rabbi, cannot forget the loss of his son. After twenty five years of his absence, he explains the reasons why he disappeared and what made him send donations every year to the local synogogue. His son is always after *goyim* because Jews are poor. They are not good enough for him. When he enters the university, he faces a consistent propaganda against Jews by a professor who made it a classroom practice to instil a sense of outrage in his students. There comes a day, when drunk with these anti-Semitic invectives, his fellow students beat up Adam. His clothes are torn and his nakedness uncovered. This experience makes him choose a different life. The Rabbi does not like to invite his son because he knows that his son is not interested in living the persecuted life of the Jews. He wants to give up his

Judaism and live with security and comfort. All this cannot prove that he finally severed his relations with Judaism. He sends donations regularly and his suicide in the last scene proves that the roots cannot be snapped for ever. Not knowing how to continue the tempestuous agony of maintaining double identities—one Jewish and the other borrowed one—he solves the crisis in the only possible way—jumping off the airplane. If the play has to conclude here it would only sound a pessimistic note. Lewisohn, being a Zionist himself, would never accept such a melancholy note. He provides an epilogue where one sees Jewish pioneers in the then Palestine slowly putting their dedicated efforts to redeem the land by cultivating land. Lewisohn conveys his message through Chaluzah:

> We're seeking a new way of life. Since we're Jews it must be a Jewish way of life. Other new way may be just as good. They wouldn't be ours. Somebody else's body or even clothes may be better than us. They couldn't fit us. And a new Jewish way of life can be sought and created only here. (97)

This play is intended to be a message to the assimilationist immigrants who, Lewisohn fears, may disappear in the American melting pot and lose their Jewish identity. This play stands out as a contrast to Israel Zangwill's *The Melting Pot* (1909). Written in the later part of the nineteenth century, the play predicts that ethnic pluralism will disappear in the melting pot. Consequently there will be only an American identity. A perspicacious Judaic scholar, Zangwill approved of this change since he vaguely felt that ethnic exclusion would once again bring the shtetl fears resulting in Pogroms. In later years, he had to revise this opinion when he was influenced by Theodore Herzl. However, Lewisohn's play contests his thesis. Though the play's locale is not exclusively in America, the message could not go unnoticed. Adam is a self-hating Jewish prototype. By presenting the crisis of his life, the author reinforced the need to feel strongly about one's own roots and make peace with his religion and advocate political Zionism.

Murray Schisgal's *The Pushcart Peddlers* recreates the overwhelming enthusiasm of the just arrived immigrants to get rich quick in America. Having heard so much about America as the land of opportunity, freedom, affluence and upward mobility, they are eager to start the moment they land in America with dreams of becoming rich. Schisgal comments on the irony of such a pursuit since it is not only difficult for a new immigrant to achieve it but it also demands a moral compromise.

Cornelius is an American name which Elias Crapavamishkes adopts because he quickly realizes that with his name, he can never reach the Americans. When Shimmel Shitzman arrives, Cornelius advises him to buy an American name. Convincingly enough, when the flower girl hears his name she not only laughs at him but also asks him to go away though he seriously wanted to help her, thinking that she is a blind girl, since their theory goes that all flower girls in America are blind. Even the flower girl, Maggie, has a dream of becoming a star in a Broadway musical. With proverbial wheeler-dealer cunning, Cornelius manages to sell his pushcart to Shimmel and takes all his money. Eager to start peddling, Shimmel starts to sell bananas immediately. In the meantime, Cornelius comes with another pushcart and bananas and effectively sells more with a skillful salesmanship. Shimmel, being a stranger at this, gets panicky because he knows he cannot compete with him. Then Cornelius asks him to beg for a compromise. Shimmel agrees and says that he has to feed the families left behind in the Old Country. They are in a pitiable situation with no proper food and clothing. They finally agree to have a just organization with sixty-forty partnership. The inhuman competition and the inevitable compromises that ensue are significant in this context. For a newcomer like Shimmel, this is an education and yet he is not discouraged. He yearns to be a millionaire, or a celebrity or a politician. He is, in fact, startled when he is asked to change his name and sadly learns that his skills as a carpenter and tinsmith will not be of any use here. Cornelius takes advantage of his predicament only because, in any case, some one else might have done the same thing to him. There are rational comments intermittently on some of the usual aspects like changing names, enquiring about their business with typical sarcasm and sales-talk.

Shimmel is pained by his inexperience especially when Cornelius successfully manages with Maggie who throws Shimmel out. Cornelius gives a dream picture to Maggie that he wants to gain a seat on the Stock Exchange and invest money on a musical comedy. Since she does not have any talent to speak of, she is completely taken in and asks him to visit her. Now Cornelius and Shimmel, the future millionaires, ask her to show her talent. She dances to their satisfaction but it is evident that she does not have any talent. And yet they praise her and ask her to practice. Shimmel admires the girl but his future partner admonishes him to be impersonal because this is the quality to cherish if one is to go ahead. With all these dream visions of becoming rich, the play ends. What is so satirical in this play is that throughout their prolonged conversation, not a single person purchases anything from them. Their conversation is syncopated with abrupt enquiries by each other as to how the business is going. Both of them, at different situations, say that it is progressing which is not true. Both of them are immigrants and they have to look after their families in the Old Country. But Shimmel says he met the girl of his dreams and forgets everything about his Old Country family. Cornelius, a married man, has a girl of his own. Schisgal brings out convincingly the inner workings of the American dream: Competition, rat race, betrayals, impersonality, golden girl myth and perpetual race to go still further. The fact that human concerns are subdued in the process, makes this play poignant while maintaining entertaining satire.

Israel Horowitz's *The Indian Wants the Bronx* portrays today's America. There is hardly anything Jewish about this play. However, Horowitz's vision of America and its stifling social atmosphere, is essentially Jewish. The biting scepticism is a common theme in many Jewish writings of contemporary America. Horowitz wrote many plays where the Jewish response to the present American system was presented. This play concentrates on urban violence and how it becomes a menacing threat to a non-

English speaking Indian to reach his son. Adopting the black humour technique, Horowitz formulates the encounter between two violent American youths—one Jewish, and another Irish—and an Indian, who knows only Hindi. In the long ordeal of Gupta, one sees the perversity of America. The verbal and physical violence of Joe and Murphy against Gupta, and between themselves, borders on subversion. The play begins with a rock-song coming offstage. Gupta is waiting at the bus-stop to go to the Bronx. The boys emerge on the stage as Joey and Murphy. Their conversation wanders from homosexual suggestions to derogatory comments on the Indian. They speak to Gupta. He responds in Hindi which they do not follow. As the play continues, their life stories are unravelled: their thievery, many shameful acts and murder. Murphy's mother is a prostitute and still cannot make a living and seems to have a liking for Joey. Murphy evidently does not like foreigners because this "city's a regular melting pot. Turkies, Kikes like you."[5] Gupta's horror increases when he sees mock-fights which take on real proportion between Joey and Murphy. Murphy's arm is savagely twisted by Joe. Again, in the last few scenes, Murphy enters and cuts Gupta's hand. Joey stands dismayed at the sight. Gupta doesn't understand their language. Joey says: "Why the hell did you come here, anyway?"[6] When they take out his address and ring his son up, not to inform that Gupta is at the bus-stop, but only to create anxiety in him, Gupta desperately moves to the booth and takes the phone and talks in Hindi. In the meantime, the phone wire is cut by Murphy. Realizing that there is no respite from this situation, Gupta hits one of them. Finally, his hand is cut and he is left alone on the stage with his bleeding hand. With pathetic hope, he talks into the phone, though its wire is cut. He shows the phone to the audience while talking into it, suggesting what America has done to him. The message to the audience is clear, that the America of affluence, opportunity and pursuit of happiness has gone to the extent of perverse levels where animalism is the common feature. Horowitz deals with the problem of urban violence and increasing intolerance in America during the sixties. A harmless man like Gupta who comes to stay with his son upon his invitation since his wife had died, cannot find peace in America. At the end of the play, he speaks a few words of English he learnt from the conversation with the gangster youth of America. And thanks the audience as if to ask whatever has happened to the American dreams.

Yale M. Udoff's *The Little Gentleman* explores yet another immigrant problem. The generation of the Old Country with the consciousness of their identity and Yiddish culture; the first generation in the process of Americanization and disgust for the Old Country values; and the third generation becoming the battleground for the conflict, each trying to assert their exclusive influence on it—these aspects become the subject matter.

It is Ronald's birthday. Mother wants to inculcate the all-American myth in him. The boy is taught to develop the British accent with a strong concern for "superior taste" in everything. Their house is adequately furnished according to modern taste. Though it is their child's birthday, Mother does not allow her husband, Harold, to come home for lunch because he is to make money. He wants to come for the birthday celebration but Mother does not allow it. The fact that the child's role is played by an adult is of significance here. It may mean that though he is fairly grown up in years, he is still treated as a child owing to Mother's excessive concern for so-called tastes of Christian culture which is suffocating to the child. Ronald's persistent question as to her Christian name suggests that though she is Jewish, she thinks she is a Christian in every attitude of her life. It makes her question her mother, Dora, a true champion of the Old World culture. When Dora gives her "Melodies of the Old World," Mother is not altogether convinced, though the phonograph impresses her to an extent. Mother gives a complete set of Beethoven records to express her faith in gentile culture. On her part, Dora teaches him some Yiddish words. Mother has plans for the child's future and feels that he should become an English nobleman or a darling American boy. But the child wants to become a bartender because bartenders are the most interesting people as TV programmes show. Dora does not approve of her daughter's obsession with American ways. As this conflict continues, Sylvia wants to see their modern apartment.

Ronald asks Dora to wheel the carriage on the terrace before she goes out to bring some cake. Before she leaves, Dora breaks the bust of Beethoven, a symbol of an alien culture which is driving her daughter and, now, her grandson away from their roots. When Ronald is taken to the terrace, he wheels himself to an edge and commits suicide. Ronald likes Yiddish songs and, in this, he shows his concern for the Old Country Yiddish culture which is a source of sustaining force for his grandparents. The anguish of sharing the ethos of two worlds with different values and cultures and the predicament to be forced to choose between them, is convincingly presented. The emotional turbulence of the process of Americanization is painful demanding enormous sacrifice, sometimes even their roots. A similar incident narrated by aunt Sylvia, confirms that the agony of being torn between Yiddish identity and the American myth is not only archetypal but also a true voice of the immigrant Jewish life in America.

Having analyzed the immigrant life, it would be worthwhile to turn to the Jewish communal life. Again, it is a contrast to the Old Country shtetl life with its self-contained values and social patterns. The interaction between Jew and gentiles brings another aspect—the possible intermarriage. These themes of intermarriage appear in 1924 in Anne Nichols's play *Abie's Irish Rose* which was immensely popular. In David Belasco's *Men and Women* this theme is presented but the marriage does not take place. Paddy Chayefsky's *Middle of the Night* has a Jewish manufacturer falling in love with a gentile in spite of protest from both sides. Again, there are problems for them, not necessarily because their religions are different but because the age disparity is so much in the father-daughter relationship. Lanford Wilson's *Talley's Folly* (1979) tells the story of a post-Holocaust Matt Friedman, whose entire family became a victim of European anti-Semitism, falling in love with a gentile, Sally Talley, after living in emotional uncertainty for forty years. They too hope to succeed in their relationship. In all these plays, the theme of intermarriage does not create controversies. Though both families have misgivings about it owing to religious differences, the lovers overcome these problems and, in the end, they are united which would not have been possible either in Yiddish literature at the turn of the century or in Jewish literature of the early part of the century. Though Israel Cohen sacrifices his love for his gentile friend, it serves more than one purpose for David Belasco: first, he succeeds in presenting Israel Cohen as a benevolent Jew, the counter-Shylock; and two, he also solves the problem of intermarriage which certainly would have created a controversy in the self-conscious years of the early immigrant Jewish life.

Anne Nichols's *Abie's Irish Rose* appears more impressive on this theme. Chayefsky's *Middle of the Night* basically concentrates on the middle-age crisis of a Jewish manufacturer whose wife died some time ago. But inter-religious relationships add to the complication, resulting in the crisis of middle age. Lanford Wilson's *Talley's Folly* has been widely appreciated by critics and got the Pulitzer prize in 1980. Whatever may be the emotional disturbances both Matt and Sally face—Matt's family's massacre and Sally's breaking off the engagement because she cannot have children—the play still fails to be consistent on certain themes. For a Post-Holocaust Jew, Matt seems to be fairly unconcerned about the consequences of the Holocaust on the Jewish psyche. His character portrayal is unconvincing. Except the information that his family is the victim of anti-Semitism, there is hardly any emotional or situational suggestiveness which can bring out the chaos of his life convincingly. Having been a victim of social and political discrimination, he still does not seem to ponder, even for a moment, that he is in love with a gentile. The usual justification for such a thing can be that either he does not know the whole historical context of the Holocaust or he is too dull-witted to have any perspective. Either way it is a poor character-portrayal. Instead, after many years of soul-searching and bachelorhood, he needs a girl who is in the same emotional state and having found her takes a chance of falling in love with her. Not surprisingly, there is resistance from her family owing to the usual stereotypical notions about the Jew. Finally, they come to an understanding with a suggestion that they may marry and start a new life altogether. Wilson tries to intersperse the play with his attempt at Jewish humour and typical Jewish syntax but one cannot say that he is always successful at it. The only non-Jewish writer who could succeed in this attempt to a certain degree is John Updike, who wrote two books with a Jewish protagonist. Both *Bech: A Book* and *Bech is Back* capture the quintessential Jewish humour with near success. Wilson does not seem to be very successful in this attempt. However, the play ends with a positive note on the theme of interreligious marriage.

Anne Nichols's *Abie's Irish Rose* is essentially about the possible consequence of the idea of interreligious marriage and sets out to analyze, with typical humour, the response to such an idea both from Jewish and Christian viewpoints. The play was written in the late nineteen twenties and as typical of that period, the play is flooded with the Yiddish accent of the Jews, which Harold Cantor calls Yinglish, Jewish humour, and the popular stereotype—the Jew as manufacturer. A play about the immigrant Jewish boy who falls in love with a gentile and marries, both in the Methodist Church and later according to Jewish customs, it has many stock situations, tricks and turns of situational comedy. Once the marriage is over according to both Christian and Jewish customs, the truth is known to the elders of both sides followed by a noisy quarrel. Consequently, the youngsters decide to stay separately. The Jewish father being what he is, goes to his son when he learns that he has a grandchild only to realize that his son is blessed with twins, male and female, and both are named after the Christian and Jewish elders. The play tries to bring both religions together and have an integrating and tolerant view, which speaks of the spirit of the times. The subsequent revivals of the play are met with disapproval from Jewish religious leaders. Some situations in the play are hurtful to the Jews. For instance, the youngster prepares both ham and kosher food in the same house and serves according to the religious convictions of Christian and Jewish grandparents. However, the play is more than Abie and Rose's marriage. It presents a forum for Jewish and Christian relations. This idea is suggested when Rabbi and priest have a friendly conversation. In three acts, the playwright makes use of cliché situations, Jewish humour, other comic types of the twenties to create a delightful comedy. The fact that many critics did not like it—the reasons are obvious on that it is not original in theme and treatment—did not stop its immense popularity. Stanley Richards, an eminent theatre critic, writes: "The phenomenon that was *Abie's Irish Rose* has never been duplicated in the American theatre. A ragbag of a play populated with an assortment of stereotype replete with lowgrade vaudeville humour and peppered with comic dialects, it nevertheless ran for 2,327 performances in New York, a record that was not to be topped until a decade later by *Tobacco Road.*"

It has greater relevance for the discussion of intermarriage than Wilson's play since it avowedly tries to treat themes as they are, and not simply create an ethnic milieu to the otherwise major theme of love between two people of different emotional set-ups, as Wilson certainly does in his play. In Chayefsky's play also the emphasis is on the middle-age crisis and the ethnic background is incidental, though it makes its own contribution to the disgruntlement and disapproval of the Jewish manufacturer's sister and the Christian girl's mother. However, the play still ends on a positive note. Of all these plays, only *Abie's Irish Rose* is significant in the sense that the theme of intermarriage is presented as the central focus and does not digress from it. The fact that the play does not have the sophisticated treatment of its theme is only too clear. What has to be noted, however, is that in all these plays, the marriages are approved though with initial embarrassment which is the source of dramatic situations. It may be surmised that ethnic differences are generally tolerated and the Jew has found a place in mainstream American social life and is being accepted as such. Though cultural and ethnic pluralism is appreciated by sociological studies, the trend towards intermarriage certainly disturbs the orthodox Jewish circles which was never a problem in the self-contained Jewish ghettoes. Though Jewish emancipation is welcomed with enthusiasm, they were ambivalent in their assessment of the problems in the post-emancipation era. However, one cannot read too much into the realistic implication of the play. The fact remains, however, that it is a matter of concern to American Judaism.

There are changing perspectives on the horizon of religious and the ritualistic front. With a growing Americanization, religious life of Jews is also affected to a certain extent especially orthodox Jewish life. It has been noted already that the Enlightenment gave rise to three Jewish religious patterns: neo-Orthodoxy, Conservative and Reform Judaism. In America, Reform Judaism is popular to a large extent with a slow decline in the membership to the Orthodox synogogues. Chayefsky's *The Tenth Man* has the Orthodox synogogue as its locale, where the entire action takes place. The synogogue, peopled with insufficient *minyan* of the old Jews, progresses to concentrate on the exorcism of the *dybbuk* which enters Evelyn Foreman's body. When the entire process of exorcism is over, the *dybbuk* (devil) flees not from the girl but from Arthur Landau—a young man who is incessantly nihilistic, already with a divorce in his life. It has many aspects of Orthodox practices like morning prayers, and afternoon prayers. In between, the story of the schizophrenic girl, cynical Arthur, the religious state of affairs at the synogogue, the transition from atheism to Jewish faith, and comments on Jewish life are told. The author believes that Jewish identity and religious faith is not only the answer to modernity but that Judaism can also accommodate modern ways of thinking and scientific knowledge.

Act One takes place in the interior of synogogue. It is oppressively cold outside, and inside a Cabalist is immersed in his prayers. Zitorsky and Schlissel start their conversation with a peculiar antagonism towards their daughter-in-law and later it focuses on Foreman's granddaughter who is put in a mental institution. Alper arrives and starts reciting prayers. But there is the usual problem of finding ten people for the congregation. The Sexton talks to the Harris and Kessler boys and requests them to come to the synogogue. In the meantime, Schlissel, the self-proclaimed atheist who is to become devout at the end, makes sarcastic comments on Hirshman's "pietistic humbug." The synogogue itself is in a ruined state and for the last few weeks there has not been a service owing to an inadequate number for the *minyan*. After some time, Foreman arrives with his granddaughter and announces that she is possessed with a *dybbuk.* As an Orthodox Jew, Foreman does not believe in the Cabala and the *Book of Zohar* is strictly prohibited because it deals with demonology and numerology and has an extreme interpretation of the Torah. And yet, having listened to Evelyn, he half-heartedly brings her to the synogogue. A certain Hannah Luchinsky whom Foreman dishonoured in her youth, dies on a sea-journey and Kaddish (prayers for the dead) is not said for her. Therefore, she is doomed to wander the earth until she finds a clean soul who can redeem her from perdition. A strongly felt Jewish belief of ghetto life, this idea is widely popular with other European Jews also. The other Jews are convinced but when Evelyn speaks about Zitorsky's extra-marital affairs and the eventual death of his wife, they begin to realize that, after all, it may be true. So, they decide to call a Miracle-worker rabbi to exorcise the *dybbuk* from her because the young rabbi of their synogogue may not be well-versed with the practice. Meanwhile, the search for the required number of people for the *minyan* continues. And the Sexton brings Arthur as the tenth man. But Arthur does not know what to do with tallith and phylacteries though he is Jewish himself. Schlissel's comments inform the situation of the American Jewish life at that time:

> Here you have the decline of Orthodox Judaism graphically before our eyes. This is a synogogue? A converted grocery store, flanked on one side by a day cleaner and on the other by a shoemaker. Really, if it was not for the Holy Ark there, this place would look like the local head quarters of the American Labor Party. In Poland, where we were all one step from starvation we had a synogogue whose shadow had more dignity than this place.[8]

While talking about the Miracle-worker, he makes pungent remarks that are typical of him. He explains the unimpressive ways of the Miracle-worker in a sarcastic manner. He concludes:

> The Mircale-worker wandered off to work other miracles and

> the mule driver sold his mule and went to America where I assume, because he was a habitual drunkard and insensitive boor, he achieved considerable success. (41)

His skepticism about America and the decline of religious importance are obvious. Arthur stands as a proof of his tirades against America. Still, he is the tenth man and as the curtain falls, the congregation is ready for the morning service. Foreman goes to fetch the rabbi and Evelyn sits in the rabbi's office.

The Second Act begins with the morning prayers. When the Kessler boy is asked to read from the Torah, he is nervous and asks someone else to read from it. There follows a conversation between Evelyn and Arthur which suggests that Evelyn is brought up in an orthodox family. She knows some theological arguments and can make intelligent comment on the rituals and the Hebrew bible. She knows that she is getting unsuccessful psychiatric help. She can objectively analyze her situation and tells him that she is "a little paranoid and hallucinates a great deal and has a very little sense of reality, except for brief interludes like this, and I might slip off any minute in the middle of a sentence into some incoherency." (66) Aurthur tells his part of the problem and his "ironic detachment" which depresses him. He left the Communist Party when he realized that there were easier ways to seduce girls. In his long confessional talks, he makes certain comments on American life as he understood it:

> Americans, you know, are frantic being happy. The American nirvana is a man and his wife watching television amiable and then turning off the light and effortlessly making the most ardent love to each other. . . . I began to work day and night at my law office, and besides becoming very successful, I managed to avoid my wife entirely. For this deceit, I was called ambitious and was respected by every one including my wife, who was quite as bored as I was with her. (70)

Arthur realizes that these old Jews are upto an exorcism and, being not a believer, he wants to liberate Evelyn from the trouble and inform her parents about this which, in turn, surprises the Cabalist and other old men. At the same time, some conversational implications among many people suggest various aspects of contemporary Jewry. For instance, the rabbi says that he was enthusiastic to preach the Torah in the beginning and sharply criticized the people who broke the Sabbath laws as a result of which his congregation dwindled. Again, the Cabalist has a dream in which his pious father calls him rabbi and tells him that he is among the righteous people though, as a child, the Cabalist "lustfully threw away the white fringed shawl of the rabbinate" (92) and mocked the law. For so many years, the Cabalist was penancing and, finally, he got the sign he was waiting for. He shares the precious moment with his companions. They sing and dance the old Hasidic dance. Arthur also participates in the rejoicing of the Cabalist but it does not stop him from worrying about Evelyn since he has acquainted himself with the girl and has begun to love her. He wants to inform her parents. The Cabalist informs him that her father must be in his Office, busy with the work-a-day activities unmindful of or indifferent to his daughter's problem. Alper finds this opportunity to air yet another vindictive theory on contemporary youth. These flashes of comments on various aspects of the Jewry are important because they throw light on the major discussion of the chapter. The Jewish dilemma with its gains and losses in the New World becomes part of the structure of consciousness behind the ambivalent attitude towards American values. The decline in the role of religion haunts the old Jews of the synogogue who have to force people to be in the *minyan*. Alper's words are suggestive of his attitude towards the change. He says:

> It is symptomatic of the current generation, Rabbi Israel, to be utterly disillusioned. Historically speaking, an era of prosperity following an era of hardtimes usually produces number of despairing and quietistic philosophies, for the new prosperous people have found out they are just as unhappy as when they were poor. Thus when an intelligent man of such a

generation discovers that two television sets have no more meaning than one or that he gets along no better with his wife in a suburban house than he did in their small city flat, he arrives at the natural assumption that life is utterly meaningless. (105)

Alper's rationalization about Arthur and his generation does not deter Arthur. The Cabalist affirms that Arthur is blindly possessed by the Tangible. Arthur hits back saying that the concept of God is fabricated by guilt-ridden people. As these arguments continue, the girl's situation gets worse. Since the Cabalist attained a stage of righteousness, he takes up the process of exorcism. Act Two ends with the uneasy uncertainty of Arthur towards the ritual.

In the Third Act, the entire ritual of exorcism is dramatized. Once again, it is a problem of needing ten people for the service due to the departure of the Kessler boys. The police is on the look out for Evelyn, having received a report from her father regarding her disappearance. Ironically, the policeman becomes the tenth man. In a short conversation between Arthur and Evelyn, she tells him that he is possessed because she senses that Arthur does not believe in anything. The Cabalist starts the ritual and the *dybbuk* is adamant in not leaving Evelyn. Finally, when the exorcism is completed, Arthur screams and falls down, suggesting that it is the *dybbuk* in him that is liberated and not the girl. However, when Arthur regains consciousness—now a new person with eventual acceptance of the religion—he decides to take care of the girl and promises that he could exorcise the *dybbuk* in her. The return of Arthur and Schlissel to their faith and the reality that the Kessler boys are not so keen and there is a regular problem of finding *minyan* for the service clearly underlines the reality of American Judaism. However there is hope as suggested in the play. The fact remains that there is a crisis in religious life in America. One can go further and say that Chayefsky's play is about Orthodox Judaism and, to that extent, the crisis may be true. Generalizing on the basis of the crisis in Orthodox Judaism the whole of the Jewish experience may not be accurate especially when the majority of the American Jews belong to Reform Judaism. Whatever may be the relevance of such a viewpoint, it should be admitted that the attitude towards American Judaism is, on the whole, alarming.

The decline of Orthodox Judaism is suggested in yet another play written by Michael Kassin entitled *Today a Little Extra*. Zalman Abrams sells his Kosher shop after owning it for thirty five years. In the long conversation between Abrams and Mark Levine, the new owner, one senses that there is a sad relaxation in the Orthodox practices of the Jewish rituals. Thus the Jewish communal life presented in the play is riddled with ambiguities. The intermarriage theme is fairly affirmed whereas the decline of Orthodox Judaism is disapproved as in *The Tenth Man*. However, even in this play, the hope for the future is not ruled out. Mark Levine, the new owner, in *Today a Little Extra* is efficient and may still practice the Kosher rituals, though there may be lapses in other Jewish Kosher shops. These changes are essentially American and even if the playwrights made them rather acceptable with some reservation, it still stands out as a contrast to the Old Country life. And this contrast, with all the arguments and counter-arguments, is still not healthy from the Jewish point of view.

The three aspects discussed so far—the prototypical Jew in the gentile world as in Adam, the immigrant hopes and actuality, the Jewish communal life—become the sustaining source for the Jewish dissent against the American dream. The lessons derived from the three aspects serve as a guiding force in the moralistic assessment of the American dream. Being humanists themselves, the materialistic perversion of the American dream bothered them. Though the plays discussed so far, according to the classified themes, can be considered as responses of the times that influence them, the essential conciliatory tone cannot be taken as an outright approval of the American experience. With the rejection of assimilationism of the melting pot concept, the affirmation and positive consciousness of Judaism becomes a factor which moulded their outlook in more ways than one. Small wonder that the Jewish writers are the most vocal dissidents of the neurotic side of the American dream. The three major dramatists who broke the myth of success are Clifford Odets, Arthur Miller and David Mamet. Their plays debunk the dream in the sense that they negate the very idea of the materialistic success which becomes the only acceptable interpretation of the American dream in modern times. There are also other characters who respond soberly to the ethics of the American dream and never face any crisis. These persons not only survive the onslaught of American materialism, but they also survive with human dignity.

Clifford Odets's *Golden Boy* (1937) is about Joe Bonaparte, of an immigrant Italian family, who wants to define himself, according to American materialism and various myths that spring from it. The play sets out to focus on what a social myth can do to a sensitive youth who wants to have a sense of belonging. Joe's identification with music and the frequent onslaught of the social myth which finally takes him from his real self and leads him to a stage where he is more receptive to the myth of success than to the inner peace which he finds in music. It also speaks of his vulnerability to be adversely affected by a social myth where there are also many people who preserve themselves or create a ring of insularity and fight against it by dedicating themselves to the values and even wage war for their relevance to humanity. The American social psyche is influenced by the Horatio Alger myth, upward mobility and the oft-quoted goal: life, liberty and the pursuit of happiness. The portrayal of Joe in *Golden Boy* is a shattering version of the pathological side of the myth. However, Joe is surrounded by a family which rejects his ambition of finding himself in success, fame and riches. His father Mr. Bonaparte and his brother Frank belong to this section which not only disapproves of the abnormal desire for success in Joe which foretells the doom he is to face and also his assertion of the very interpretation of success in materialistic terms. Joe becomes a pugilist which, in turn, makes him successful, rich and famous. But his conscience-pricking never allows him peace and he immediately realizes that for his manager, Moody, he is simply a "gold mine" and for Eddie he is a means to show that he can beat America on its own terms. Since Eddie cannot be a champ, he has to find a surrogate who can be one, and thus identify himself with him in a vicarious need to have a self-justification. Eddie is a tough "guy" in a tough American milieu and he does not care about money as long as Joe can win in the ring. Having reached the stage of the mythical golden boy, Joe must have a golden girl. He takes Moody's girl, Lorna. The competitiveness is inhuman and Joe is well-tuned to the ethic of competition. Lorna tells him that she is liberated from her miseries by Moody and yet with a little persuasion she escapes with Joe. The fact that her marriage with Moody is fixed does not bother her. The golden boy wins the golden girl and the streak of success has to end in the inevitable car crash. Joe's success is amazing and yet that he suppressed his instinctive love for music which alone gives him a sense of harmony, stands as a disquieting force. Compared to the success story of Joe, Frank's role is not adequately developed. However, Frank's comments assume a certain significance since he is the anti-thesis of Joe's obsessions. He is a union leader and he fights for the rights and benefits of the people. Though he does not have the riches of Joe, he is at home with his conscience: "The pleasure of acting as you think! The satisfaction of staying where you belong, being what you are . . . at harmony with millions of others!"[9] In the mid-thirties being a unionist is the most glorified cause especially at a time, when being a Communist meant not only a voice against the bourgeoisie but also against the malady that results from bourgeoisie values of which Joe is certainly a victim. When he receives the news of Joe's death, his response is simply: "What waste!"[10]

Odets as a social dramatist hardly needs to be commented upon. His criticism of American materialism is vehement in all of his plays. *The Big Knife* figures in the same category where he talks about the corruption of personality as an inevitable process in the American system. He tried to attack the system which glorifies the "bitch goddess success" and "money," "status," "fame" that contribute to it. These terms are used and understood in a different way. Richard M. Huber elaborates on it:

Success was not earned by being a loyal friend or good

husband. It was a reward for performance on the job. It is not the same thing as happiness—which is how you feel. Success was brutally objective and impersonal. It recorded a change in rank, the upgrading of a person in relation to others by the unequal distribution of money and power, prestige and fame. Yet success was not simply *being* rich or famous. It meant *attaining* riches or *achieving* fame. You had to know where a man began and where he ended in order to determine how far he had come.[11]

Joe fails to make a distinction between success and happiness. His false belief that money, status, fame should give a sense of belonging and an identity has the seed of disintegration in itself. His death does not come as à surprise to Mr. Bonaparte and Frank. Mr. Bonaparte tells Lorna to teach Joe that truthful success is different from the pugilist's success. The fact, that Frank is presumed as an anti-thesis to Joe, cannot be overemphasized in terms of dramaturgy. Frank is an insignificant character in the play. He is one of the members of the family, and he has his own way of responding to the American values. The play is predominantly about Joe's life. Odets does not give enough importance to Frank which might have given a theoretical strength to the play's theme. Odets certainly approves and exalts Frank's view and it is the weakness of the play that Frank does not occupy the kind of role that could have contributed to a convincing measure in terms of the affirmed views of Odets. One can also interpret this lapse as a playwright's priority since he is concerned with the success and fall of Joe Bonaparte. He is not even a tragic figure since he does not have inexplicable circumstances to be fought against nor does he make an attempt to do so. On the other hand, he accepts the dictates of the social circumstances and tries to redefine himself within its purview. The failure to make Frank an adequate character makes it impossible to establish the only claim the play purports to have: a social message that American success destroys what is good in man and Frank is an embodiment of human dignity who rejects the success-myth.

The neurosis of the American dream is projected, with more

consistency and complexity both in dramaturgy and in symbolic terms, in Arthur Miller's *Death of a Salesman*. The profession of the salesman epitomizes initiative, drive, ambition, competitive spirit, and an urge to be always at the top—a number one man. A profession which alludes to the upward mobility and changing social ranks, it has developed its own ethic and system of priorities over the years. The Franklinesque emphasis on character, industry, perseverance and ambition as the essential backdrop to the rags-to-riches mobility of the average American is replaced by the notorious sales talk of ad-culture, personality, good looks and handsomeness and the destroying of the competitor through all means. When the American dream is negated, it is also in terms of the redefinition of the success-myth of the latter version. In this version the human factor, relationships and loyalties of any kind, do not figure. What matters is the utility of a person or the contribution of a person to organizational progress.

Willy Loman in Arthur Miller's play is an average American, brought up on the All-American myth. His speeches are filled with appreciations and accolades of America and its various patterns. For him the Chevrolet is the best American car and he is mystified at the fact that his son, Biff, is lost in America—the greatest country on earth. He associates all the qualities that sell with his son Biff—he is Adonis and Hercules, embodying initiative, drive, personality and, most importantly, the quality of being not only liked but well-liked. Willy Loman honestly believes in all these things, hoping that they contribute to the upward mobility of a person. When Biff steals volley-ball, he calls it initiative and hence acceptable. He thinks that if any other boy did such a thing, the coach would surely take action against him. But Biff is a special person since he has a charming personality which makes all the difference. The fact that nothing has happened despite the offense amply proves for Willy that Biff's personality sells which conforms to the American myth. Even so, Willy—not being a man of high thinking though with an inner voice—is a confused man. Though Linda, his wife, does not appreciate Biff's lapses, Willy continues to tolerate them. If he indulges in All-American talk and appreciates the dream of success, it is not always voluntary for he keeps wondering if he is teaching his children the right values. In his fantasies, he asks his brother for his advice regarding these matters because he always feels "temporary." Willy Loman is a man of infinite contradictions. He contradicts his own statement with no effort and, more significantly, he is probably unaware of it. These contradictions speak about his psychological state and his indecisive response to social values. The intermittent flute music, the fantasies where he has conversations with Ben, and his agrarian vision underline a different personality of Willy Loman. This version of him is an anti-thesis to the All-american myth he fervently infuses into the minds of his children. Willy never had concrete memories of his father and the flute music of his father, who used to go from place to place to sell flutes in the true American tradition of the frontier spirit and adventure, dimly suggests his inner urge to re-experience his childhood days where a protective intimacy could be possible between him and his father. In other words, he feels the absence of roots and hence the foundation which can stand him in good stead and provide security. And he says to Ben that he feels "temporary." The American tradition of emphasizing the stock one comes from is denied to him. When he ultimately realizes that Biff's failure to achieve success is due to his adulterous relationship which destroys his son's faith in Willy as the guiding parent and, in particular, a symbol of what Biff has come to idealize, Willy Loman subconsciously realizes that he is absenting himself from the world of his children. The flute music probably connects symbolically the psychological trauma of Willy Loman. Further, to be successful, there has to be both a change in ranks and the benefit of the stock one came from. This causes guilt-feeling in him and he feels that Biff detests him for his lapse. Also, Biff's success is important to him since it would reassure him that he is not effaced from his world. His constant enquiries about Biff's improvement and his enthusiastic All-American talk in the hope of finding an opportunity for Biff may have personal implications to Willy, evocative of his need for personal redemption.

However, Biff is a different man. Encouraged when he stole

the volley-ball as a child, Biff finds it part of his life to steal something or anything and he believes that he may be right after all in doing so. The fact that his father now admonishes him against such practices vehemently, makes him wonder if he is on the right path to achieve his dream. In fact, Bernard keeps informing Willy about the consequences. But Willy cannot convince himself that hard work is important and personal attraction does not always pay. Willy glories in that Biff is not only liked but well-liked and a person with that distinction can never fail to make the grade. Sure enough, Biff is liked by the coach, the girls and everybody. He has the drive and he is a captain in the ballgame. These achievements affirm Willy's faith in personality. Also, he gets a scholarship from three different universities for graduate programme. Willy considers Bernard as a pest, though for a moment he advises Biff to work hard. Nevertheless, Biff fails and is detained. He could have made up in the summer course but Willy's adulterous life becomes a stumbling block emotionally bringing up the question of the validity of the idealized version of Willy and the American myth he infused in his children. From then on, Biff is a changed man, probably due to a retrospective analysis of the past and an objective assessment of the American dream which his father had accepted unquestioningly so far. Strangely enough, Willy consistently harps on the agrarian vision. Willy says: "There is no breath of fresh air in the neighborhood. The grass does not grow any more, you cannot raise a carrot in the backyard. They should've had a law against apartment houses. Remember those two beautiful elmtrees out there? When I and Biff hung the swing between them."[12] And he thinks about those days of "lilac and wisterias," peonies and daffodils. He feels that the increasing urbanization destroyed the neighbourhood. He cannot grow even a carrot. While going to New England, he says, he opened the window screen and allowed himself to be bathed by fresh air. He dreams of finding some place in the country and probably raise carrots or plant seeds. Before his death, he buys seeds and desperately plants them in the backyard. The failure of America as Eden, which is also part of the Edenic themes of the American dream, is unmistakable in the troubled search of Willy for the agrarian vision which is also shared by Biff. He dreams of farming and having a ranch of his own which Willy, in his characteristic self-contradictory way, disapproves. Finally when Biff tells him to forget the "phony dream" and start living as they are and cries unashamedly. Willy is baffled and does not know why he is crying. Having reassured himself that Biff does not hate him, he prepares himself for the supreme sacrifice, once again affirming his faith in the American dream. He deliberately crashes his car with the genuine hope that the insurance money he leaves behind will work as a first step for Biff in his quest for success. The death of Willy, the Salesman, is a story fogged with helpless dreams and ironic social reality. The society that encourages his dreams also works as a suicidal undercurrent in his life for he does not assess the inner workings and the conveniences of the dream, being an average American that Willy certainly is. He believes unquestioningly although as a loving husband and father, he deeply questions its implicit savagery. This conflicting attitude is the only rationale for the troubled dreams which reveal a different person unique in many ways. His many queries indicate his inner misgivings about the myth he believes in. He dies in affirming it which speaks of the neurotic version of the success.

Biff is an extension of Willy in many ways. Brought up on the fervent glorification of American values of Willy, he thinks stealing is not a crime but symbolic of his initiative. Happy is moderately successful and a regular philanderer. When Biff meets Bill Oliver, only to make an attempt to start all over again, he cannot but steal his fountain pen. While running back with it, he stops for a moment to think about the ignominious act. He realizes that one does not have to climb the ladder of success and one can also live a peaceful life whatever one's achievement may be. He explains his realization to his father with a hope that he may admit the hypocrisy of the perpetual evasion and face up to the facts. Willy takes it as a gesture of affection. Biff also shares Willy's agrarian vision and he longs for it anxiously and yet he feels unsure of himself because he is not getting anywhere. And he asks himself: "What the hell am I doing, playing around with horses, twenty-eight dollars a week? I'm thirty-four years old, I oughta be makin' my future. That's when I come running home. And now, I get here, and I don't know what to do with myself.''[13] The conflict within makes him feel uncertain. The Edenic myth against the competitive world with its allurements of upward mobility goes against America as Eden. After his failure at starting all over again, he realizes his limitations and his real self. Significantly, he feels that one has to accept oneself and he does not have to be a successful man for it. Willy's wife, Linda, also shares this attitude when she justifies Willy and asks his children to pay more attention to him because he will get no salary after a lifetime of service to the organization which does not provide a job in New York despite his consistent request. Linda affirms the dignity of Willy.

Happy meets the American myth on its own terms and competes with a characteristic aggressiveness, ruthlessness, and manipulation. He cannot brook any higher authority. He wants to destroy the boss by any means and feels that he should prove to others that he is as good as any one else.

Uncle Ben is the symbol of success to Willy and he figures in his fantasies regularly. Willy Loman's family and their lives in various situations work as a negative side of the American dream. When Willy commits suicide, no one comes to his funeral and Willy always believed in the great American cities and the American myth. Even more ironic is that Linda does not feel that he is dead. For her, it is one of his trips to New England after all. The debunking of the American dream is complete.

Charley's and Bernard's roles give a different picture. Charley never seems to react competitively to the myth of upward mobility nor does he bring Bernard up to be a blind believer in any myth. And yet Charley is successful in his own way. Bernard becomes a lawyer and goes to argue at the Supreme Court. They made the grade without the obsessive and inhuman props that entangle the Loman family. While Happy accepts the demands whole-heartedly Willy Loman and Biff have implicit doubts about this and hence the reason for Willy's dreams and Biff's idealization of the simple agrarian life. Charley and Bernard are important in the play since they achieve success. Miller's ambivalent attitude towards the American dream is significant here. Though Charley and Bernard's achievements can be interpreted as the affirmation of the American dream, one cannot overstate this factor since the play is about Willy Loman and his tryst with the American myth. While they are never enamoured of the dream to an extent that they have to stake their personal values, it should also be understood that they seem to have an enlightened attitude towards it with a sense of sobriety. On the other hand, a salesman, whose life is filled with the positive talk of the American cliché epithets, has a possibility of making a mistake of believing in it especially if he is an ordinary man, as Willy surely is. It can also be said that in the long years of experience of Willy so much has changed in the American organizational structure. With the possible advent of ad-culture, the old style salesman is out of step with the times. The organizational system, which has no respect for the people who cannot contribute to the growth of it, ruthlessly ignores the humanistic demands of Willy. People like Willy do not figure in the hierarchy of such a system.

The ambivalence is there in *All my Sons* (1947) too. Again, Joe Keller has family loyalties and he interprets his achievements according to the well-being of his family. He does not consider the world as a family and other children as sons. Therefore, the selling of defective parts to the government does not trouble his conscience, though in his soul-searching conversation he says that he has never believed for a moment that the government would use them. His pilot-son, Larry, deliberately crashes to death after the knowledge that his father is involved in this malicious business ethics. Joe's sons believe in universal values. There they become antithetical to Joe's values. Their responsibility is to humanity and not to the family alone. However, Joe has his justifications too. He is getting old and he does not get opportunities again to do something for his children. Also, once the stigma is attached to his business owing to a failure to deliver goods at the right time, which is why he had to deliver faulty goods, his lifetime of efforts would go in vain. He takes a chance, and becomes a rich man. He did this for his children and his family. In the intense argumentative emotion, Joe bursts out saying that if he has to go to jail half of America should go to jail. What worries Chris is that he always felt that his father was better than others. He argues and makes his father realize that there is a larger family than their own and the people who died in the war are his children too. Joe realizes this and goes into the room only to put a bullet in his head. The transition from Joe, the All-American businessman to Joe, the man belonging to humanity at large, is significant. True enough, as in the Willy Loman play, the crisis of Joe and his urge for making money does not pre-occupy the other characters, for instance, his neighbours. The brother of Larry's love is a successful lawyer but he never had to resort to inhuman methods. They are fairly successful but they never had to destroy others for their achievement which is not the case in Joe's life. Here we see a positive strain in terms of the dream. Whereas Willy does not realize this nor is he even dimly aware of this, Joe shows certainly a sign of realization. And yet, the questioning spirit of Chris and Larry and Joe's business philosophy are two different approaches altogether.

Both Willy and Joe are average people with no exceptional intelligence. They accept the American myth and its demands in their own way. Willy probably feels a sense of uncertainty as to his affirmation of the myth and does not achieve it, though Joe not only affirms single-mindedly but also achieves success only to be forced to realize that his success is a failure since it does not have loyalties to the human concerns. And both Willy and Joe represent failures as fathers. They are idealized by their children though they fail to live up to their expectations which causes tension and in Biff's case a total reconsideration of his life and a shift in attitude. The protection, order, security and values an archetypal father should represent are never fulfilled by them though they are loving fathers. They fail in humanistic values. They cherish wrong dreams and pay a severe price. The father-son syndrome is purposeful: sons against fathers only on the basis of their personal convictions. And their value based priorities can be interpreted in terms of the social myth and realities. The fathers believe in the social myths interpreted in a materialistic sense devoid of human interest and the sons reject this approach and replace it with a humanistic ethic as the touchstone for the ratiocination of any myth. Whatever may be the levels of interpretations, the ambivalence and the attendant neurosis due to the unconditional acceptance of the American myth cannot be ignored. At the same time, the affirmation of the American dream is also present in the plays as has been already discussed at length. Miller seems to advocate a sober view of the American dream with an emphasis on and concern for liberal values. This is the reason why, the marginal success of the minor characters appears to be conforming to the deeply-felt vision of Miller. He rejects the neurotic after-effects of the obsessive American dream.

In recent American drama, two playwrights have explored the idea of the American dream, touching the decline of the family as a sacred institution in providing a refuge and security in the otherwise American waste land which is a major theme in Horowitz's plays. In David Mamet's case, the inhuman means the myth seems to demand is highlighted. Mamet's plays ruthlessly touch the degeneration that the dream seems to force people into. *American Buffalo* is a subversion of the American vision. Even among such swindlers and hold-upniks like Don, there is the necessity of some kind of loyalty. But this loyalty can be pushed aside in the wake of some profitable association which explains the competitiveness that sacrifices every conceivable human virtue and loyalty. Mamet's Pulitzer winning *Glengarry Glenross* (1984) dramatizes the genesis of any achievement in the case of those who succeed. Others like Shelly Levene, desperately struggle and stumble to "make it," and yet cannot. Shelly, now fallen on rough times, asks for help:

> Those guys *lived* on the business I brought in. They *lived* on it . . . and so did Murray, John. You were here you'd ve benefited from it too. And now I'm saying this. Do I want charity? Do I want *pity?* I want *sits*. I want leads don't come right out of a *phone book.* Give me a lead hotter than that, I'll go in and close it. Give me a chance. That's all I want. I'm going to *get* up on that fucking board and all I want is a

chance. It's a streak and I'm going to turn it around (pause) I need your help (pause).[14]

Shelly, once a prominent salesman, now demands not charity but useful "sits" so that he can successfully "close" the deals which, hopefully, may turn the "streak" and make him once again the famous Shelly that he has been known as. But business ethics can only think about the profit-giving sources. And Shelly is no longer "The Machine" of big success. When he senses that nothing can come out of his arguments, he arranges a hold-up at the office and later the documents are stolen. Eventually, Shelly is caught and hustled into the room for interrogation. Mamet is known for his effective use of language which is evident in this play. Behind the facade of obscene language coupled with the salesman's jargon, the vulnerability of these people and their anxiety to meet the terms so that they can once again feel secure can be perceived. The struggle they wage appears to be an ongoing turmoil for them. What the organization and the business boss does not seem to understand is that apart from their utility to them, they also have their own lives and families to think about and therefore, a bad streak in one's performance should be viewed with a sense of sympathy. In the absence of it, Shelly had to resort to unlawful means for he has to take care of his daughter and provide for her. In the character of Shelly, the agony of the salesman—Willy Loman comes to mind immediately—is compassionately portrayed. At the close of the play, Aaronow aptly says: "Oh. God. I hate this job."[15] The lack of the human factor is painful to him.

Mamet also wrote some plays where the break-up of the American family is used to suggest, in this he is essentially Jewish, that without this protective institution, modern man is left with no consoling refuge to fall back on in competitive times. He concerns himself with the theme of father-son or father-daughter relationship in *A Life in Theatre* (1977) and *Reunion* (1981). In the former an older actor, Robert, acts as a surrogate father to the young, John. In the latter play, the daughter comes to see her father after many years because she feels a sense of void and hence she needs her father. Old age needs to come to terms with life and even death with possible humour and the inevitable need to have certain illusions to bear life with endurance and dignity. These become the central themes in *Duck Variations* (1971). Horowitz, too, concerns himself with these themes in *The Former One-on-One Basket Ball Champion* (1981) and *Stage Directions* (1977) especially the latter where we see what happened to the once cohesive family. The break-up of family, they seem to suggest, is also, at least indirectly, a comment on the perversion of the American dream. Mamet seems to advocate a sense of togetherness and for Horowitz, it is the tragedy of the times in American liberalism, that constitutes his subject matter.

Mamet and Horowitz, unlike their fore-runners, vehemently attack the American myth. In the works of Odets, Miller and other Jewish playwrights of the thirties, their demythologizing of the dream is not without its regenerative aspect. In fact they seem to bemoan the loss of the conventional Franklinesque interpretation of the dream where the importance of character and adherence to personal values is honoured. Eventually, they became fruitful means of the realization of the dreams as reflected in the rags-to-riches heroes of the Horatio Alger myth. In recent Jewish American drama, the regenerative aspect of the dream is completely shunned. This reconsideration is possibly effected owing to the general failure of liberal temper in Europe and a prolonged social hierarchy which is not always built on justice and industry. In this context, Jewish American literature acted as a social seismograph registering the changing view towards the dream with an eloquent portrayal of the injustice and moral bankruptcy of the American Scene. As is clearly evident in the arguments put forth in the chapter, the diversified views towards the dream can only be explained in terms of a characteristic moral and ethical stance which becomes an integral part of the humanistic vision, which the Jewish writers in America undoubtedly expound in their creative writing as well as sociological work.

NOTES

1. Harry Roskolenko, "America, The Thief," *The Immigrant Experience,* ed. Thomes Wheeler (Baltimore: Penguin, 1971), p. 152.
2. Mary Antin, *The Promised Land* (Boston: Houghton Mifflin Company, 1912), p. XIV.
3. Abraham Cahan, *The Rise of David Levinsky* (New York: Harper Torchbooks, 1917, 1960), p. 530.
4. Ludwig Lewison, *Adam* (New York: Harper, 1929), p. 7.
5. Israel Horowitz, *The Indian Wants the Bronx, The Best Short Plays* (New York: Chilton Book Company, 1969), p. 17.
6. *Ibid.*, p. 23.
7. Stanley Richards, *The Most Popular Plays of the American Theatre* (New York: Stein and Day, 1979), p. 161.
8. Paddy Chayefsky, *The Tenth Man* (New York: Random House, 1960), p. 40.
9. Clifford Odets, *Golden Boy, Six Plays* (New York: Random House, 1939), p. 318.
10. *Ibid.*, p. 321.
11. Richard M. Huber, *The American Idea of Success* (New York: McGraw, 1971), p. 1.
12. Arthur Miller, *Death of a Salesman, Collected Plays* (New York: The Viking Press, 1957), pp. 134-35.
13. *Ibid.*, p. 139.
14. David Mamet, *Glengarry Glenross* (New York: Gross Press, 1964), p. 22.
15. *Ibid.*, p. 108.

For the Sake of Man: Jewish Commitment and the Liberal Crisis

Originating as a term from a Spanish political party called ''Liberals'' in the early 19th century, liberalism has gained wide currency in the English language. But neither the ideas it implies nor the social gospel it preaches can be decisively attributed to the Spanish political party. The ideas can be traced much further back to Judeo-Christian and Greek thought. The Hebrew Bible abounds in episodes where the relevance of liberty, liberation and social justice with an essential focus on community are repeatedly stressed. For contemporary Judaism, which inherited the enthusiastic interpretation of the Prophets by the Jews who later came into the category of Reform Judaism in the wake of Enlightenment liberal thought,it is a reflection of traditional Jewish values. This view in recent years came up for vigorous reassessment. However, one cannot ignore the efforts of *maskilim*, the liberal Jews, who preached the acceptance of Enlightenment, for they fervently believed that at last the Jewish integration was at hand. The genesis of such hopes is generally traced to Hebraic sources. Christianity, in many ways, is an extension of the Jewish tradition. Starting as a Jewish sect with Jewish converts, it built its rationale within the dictates of the law. The Protestant Reformation once again continues the spirit of man and individualism imbued in the Scriptures. In Greek tradition the oft-quoted instance of Socrates in sacrificing his life for the sake of the truth is symptomatic of man's faith in free will. The Stoics evidently established a claim that man as an individual was different from the civic pattern. The congenial atmosphere ushered in by the Renaissance decisively effected a shift from a God-centred universe to the here and now. In this context, the following instance becomes meaningful. In the proverbial story Giovanni, a thinker of the late fifteenth century, says that the Creator gives free will to man and reminds him that it is in man's hands that the strength and conviction to make a better world rests. The Creator tells Adam: "I have given thee neither a fixed abode nor a form that is thine alone nor any function peculiar to thyself, Adam, to the end that, according to thy longing and according to thy judgment, thou mayst have and possess that abode, that form, and those functions which thou thyself shall desire. The nature of all other things is limited and constrained within the bounds of law prescribed by me: thou, coerced by no necessity, shalt ordain for thy self the limits of thy nature in accordance with their free will, in whose land I have placed thee. . . . Thou shalt have the power to degenerate into the lower form of life, which are animal: thou shalt have the power, out of thy soul's judgment, to be reborn into the higher form of life, which are devine."[1] The liberalist ideas largely conform to the idea communicated here. Man as an evacuator and maker of his own future is at the heart of liberalism which, in other words, glorifies individualism. In this instance, God appears to be benevolent and paternal. The Greek philosopher presents almost the same ideas but on a non-theological base. He also projects man as the measure of things but here man is surrounded by a hostile environment. However, the emphasis is unmistakably on man and whatever he is, it is entirely upto his own doing or undoing.

Liberalist thought is not something new in the Hebraic tradition since the idea of liberty and liberation are part of the Hebrew scriptures. In fact, in most of the Jewish festivals and Rabbinic teachings, the sense of liberation either from external and even imperial forces or the tolerance towards the strangers's needs have been valued as cherished ideals and one can always argue that the relevance of these virtues are always within the confines of Judaism. The humanism preached by the Hebrew scriptures and the Talmudic works are the fountain-head for many latter-day humanistic thinkers of Jewish origin with a varying range that includes Marx, Marcuse, Morris R. Cohen, Trilling and Erich Fromm. In fact, Erich Fromm gives a radical interpretation of the Bible in *You shall Be as Gods,* making a case for radical humanism. However, it is the Reformation which decisively broke the myth of the Catholic power-structure by effecting a separation of the Church from the state which eventually stopped, to a certain extent, the religious persecution, severe punishment for the non-conformists, and finally, the arbitrary use of power in the name of religion. The Renaissance concern for the dignity of man coupled with the history and the impact of the Reformation ultimately paved the way for the Enlightenment or the Age of Reason. The French Revolution and Cartesian philosophy contributed mightily in shifting the emphasis from the God-centred universe to the man-centred universe. An increasing faith in tolerance, social justice and secularization became the true heritage from which liberalism gained major inspiration. With these factors as a focal point, liberalism strongly professed man's role in his development and the betterment of his environment. Consequently, the concepts such as individualism, a marginal governmental interference, *laissez-faire,* and liberty have developed as the guiding forces to implement the liberal principles. Later in the nineteenth century, the English utilitarians gave it the measure of philosophy. Otherwise liberalism is considered mainly to be a temper rather than an ideology. The ramification and modification in the outlook of liberal creeds are numerous in the twentieth century and many revisionist attitudes have become respectable. But these issues will be discussed in the later part of the argument.

The Jewish response to liberal thought has already been touched upon in the beginning of the presentation. Besides the scriptural sources, the centuries of persecution and ghetto-life have only made them more humanistic in their assessments. They saw in it not only liberation from the ghetto life but also a universal brotherhood, free of pogroms and persecution. The Enlightenment was welcomed by many prominent Jewish thinkers. Their works, though not always appreciated, reflect their liberal views. Thus, Moses Mendelsohn can be called the foremost liberal thinker who also became eventually the father of Reform Judaism. Morris Raphael Cohen[2] calls Spinoza the prophet of liberalism. Leo Strauss[3] imbued with the benevolence of the liberal spirit, makes an attempt to explain the liberal thought in Maimonides's *The Guide of the Perplexed.* Leo Strauss discusses *The Guide* in terms of a liberalist creed underlining the assumption that Maimonides's Jewish theological exposition convincingly explicates on what was later called liberalism in the modern period.

Jewish attraction to liberalism could be explained on many levels. Most important of all, it guarantees tolerance, individualism, and assuredly the separation of the Church and the State—all these aspects give the Jew the right to be what he is and practise his ethnic identity, though more orthodox sections of Judaism could easily see the danger in the apparent freedom granted by the Enlightenment and its outcome, liberalism. They saw disintegration in the Jewish faith in the excessive admiration for freedom and tolerance. The fact remains that liberalism—and the consequent democracy—gave Jews an opportunity which hardly has a parallel in the long history of persecution. The argument that liberalism had its source in the Enlightenment which openly expressed the need for the separation of the Church and state and extolled the Age of Reason which eventually became an inspiring forum for the secular apotheosis of man, is unquestioned in its truth. The Age of Reason also helped thinking gentiles like Gotthold Lessing[4] to look at the Jewish question sympathetically and, to a large extent, without any religious bias. When they criticized Jews, as Voltaire certainly did, they did so not because of the age-old Christian stereotypical views but as individuals with a certain religious background or belonging to a certain ethnic community, which in the long process shifted the focus onto a different level that is to help liberate the religious, economic and ethnic prejudices. It is little wonder, then, that many Jewish writers viewed these developments with enthusiasm. In fact, it becomes a backdrop for their creative writing. The emergence of the Jewish writer and his sympathetic audience outside his fellow Jews is largely made possible by these changes in every sphere of life. Although it is true that some Jewish writers, either consciously or unwittingly, introduced ethnically anonymous characters in their works, one cannot miss the essential Jewish sensibility communicated in their writings. Whatever may be the reason for their ethnic anonymity, the conflict these characters face are viewed and, therefore, presented against or in response to the background of liberalism. Increasingly, the crisis of liberalism figures predominantly in recent Jewish American literature. The various revisions of liberalism and the abuse in putting it into practice have an adverse effect on individual as has been brought into focus. In fact, one could even argue that the enthusiastic Jewish radicalism in the thirties, often embracing what they understood as Communism, is an extreme reaction to what they felt as the failure of liberalism. At the same time, Jews are conscious that it is the Enlightenment and liberal atmosphere which paved the transition from the defined patronage of ethnic literature, written for the Jews and essentially within the confines of the Jewish tradition with nationalist mornings, to the mainstream which is not only reciprocal but also mutually enriching. The Jews gained acceptance in the gentile world, but even here one cannot overlook the fact that they always interpreted the gentile world in terms of Jewish humanism.

With this background in view, in this chapter, an attempt has been made to analyze mainly the works of three major American Jewish playwrights and their response to the liberal crisis. Clifford Odets, Lillian Hellman and Arthur Miller epitomize the Jewish critique of liberalism. They also articulate the myth of American liberalism and its decline in contemporary America. Odets is the spokesman of the thirties reflecting the radical voice of Communist fervour during the Depression which, by its popularity and acceptance, can be called a negation of the liberal creed. His works also become the symbolic modes for the rise and fall of what is universally called proletarian literature. Coming into prominence in the thirties, he quickly made use of the ethos in his plays. At least, two of his plays directly refer to Communism as the only redeeming ideology for the troubled humanity. Placed in Germany, *Till the Day I Die* depicts the perils of totalitarian methods of coercion to subjugate the humanistic comrades who wage war against Nazism to save mankind from the hysteria of mass psychosis systematically propagated by Nazis in the name of nationalism and racism. In the seven scenes, the play elucidates the subversive measures of Nazi totalitarianism against underground comrades who take up the cause of demolishing the false propaganda spread by Nazis in the government-supported press. The main characters of the play are Ernst, Carl and Tilly. In the process of the play, one finds informers, conscience-stricken converts, Nazi torture-chambers, and significantly, self-sacrificing comrades. Although Ernst and his commanders continue their efforts to educate workers on the reality of the German economic collapse, which is prudently covered by the Nazi press, it is a gigantic task to face the mighty Nazi system. Once the Nazis take the comrades prisoners, they are tortured to force them into naming names and other secrets. Also, they have their own informers planted in the circle of comrades. Once Ernst is taken prisoner, the false stories about him are spread around and these the other comrades predictably believe. Ernst himself finds one Major who is a guilt-conscious comrade-turned-Nazi Officer. Married into a family of a long Nordic lineage, he is forced to live the life of a Nazi. However, he helps Ernst in divulging important information and even destroys official files for their protection. He also reminds Ernst of the impossible task of withstanding Nazi torture: "It is possible you may forget your proletarian task. . . . A man's made of flesh and bone. They'll inform your comrades through subversive means that you've turned stool pigeon. Before you know it, your own unit papers will be passing the word along. In a few months—no friends, no home." True enough, Ernst is trapped in the same circumstances. The Major's past association with radical activities is taken advantage of by another Nazi Officer. When the moment of tension becomes unavoidable, the Major kills Schlegel who keeps asking searching questions about his past. Having committed an inescapable act, he decides to give freedom to Ernst so that he can join his comrades and help the movement to continue in its struggle. The former comrade in him resurfaces and asks Ernst to build up the strength of the Red Front or the United Front. Ernst comes back only to learn the sad news from Tilly, who carries his child, that the party is to blacklist Ernst. In the party meeting, Ernst's own brother Carl makes an announcement that the party is above all fraternal compassion. While discussing the sacrifice of the Nazi-victims, the members decide to blacklist Ernst. So many party members are taken to the detention camps by the Nazis and are killed while allegedly trying to escape. Their sacrifices cannot be risked for the sake of Ernst. In the final scene, Carl and Tilly review the situation. Carl realizes that "nothing is too good for the proletariat." No one is willing to believe that he is without blemish. He explains how the Nazis spread the trap. Carl tells him that the Nazis have killed him already. He takes the clue and before he kills himself he makes prophetic comments which are part of any agit-prop play: "But we live in the joy of a great coming people! The animal kingdom is past. The day must follow the night. Now we are ready: we have been steeled in a terrible fire, but soon all the desolate places of the world must flourish with human genius. Brothers will live in the soviets of the world! Yes a world of security and freedom is waiting for all mankind."[5] These words spoken, he goes in and kills himself. But this cannot be interpreted as cynicism since Tilly carries his child for the new world guaranteed by Communism. Odets, an American Jew living in a liberal country, views Communism as a logical alternative to coercive totalitarianism which, in itself, should not be paradoxical, once the American reality in the Great Depression is taken into account. For many Americans the Wall Street Crash of 1929 is a symbolic failure of liberalism and the manipulatory strategies of Big Business. At a time when liberalism should have provided a force against totalitarian elements, it failed miserably leaving a shambles everywhere. In fact, they gained their rhetoric from its failure, and Russia, just after the Revolution, appeared to be the only substitute that can take on the responsibility for the protection of freedom. Being Jewish himself, Odets must have seen a threat in Nazi racism, which was not only being listened to with attention but also agreed to, much to the fear of German Jews. Once Odets made up his mind, his tryst with communism continued, in technically a better and moving play entitled *Waiting for Lefty* which brought him the recognition he was looking for.

Once again he focusses on the conflict between Communism and other dehumanizing ideologies. In *Till the Day I Die,* Communism is pitted against totalitarianism and in *Lefty*, it seeks to debunk the inhuman forces that suck the life of common people. These forces flourish in the liberal democracy of America which, in principle, gives excessive freedom to capitalists who go to any extent in order to gratify their greed for money. Using the expressionist techniques effectively, Odets gives authenticity and brings life-size characters who tell of their troubled lives to the audience. The cliché agit-prop for once achieves a genuine human dimension. The dramatic technique adopted by the playwright is well-suited to the theme of the unity of workers of the world. The distinction of the proscenium disappears and the actors are as real as the audience itself. The turbulent decade is presented in its microcosm where the capitalist is presented as the evil man. The play opens with the workers sitting in a semi-circle. Fatt, who wants to diffuse their plan to go on strike for better wages, is obviously a "stool pigeon." One after another, the workers come forward and tell their personal crises caused by the social malady. And their lives are enacted. Thus, Joe cannot feed his children and his wife is ready to walk out on him. A meek person, he is enlightened by his wife to see the exploitation of his employer. Whenever crucial comments are made the workers sitting in the semi-circle act as chorus. In the lab assistant's episode, Miller, the doctor, is asked by the industrialist to not only produce poison-gas for the next war but also spy on the scientist he will be working with. Florence and Sid cannot marry because they cannot make a decent living. On the other hand, the evil strategies of the Capitalist who purchases the loyalties of some gullible workers also is revealed. Benjamin, who is an efficient doctor but Jewish, loses his job to accommodate a senator's son. The whole story sums up the malignant side of Capitalism. The boss, industrialist, the senator—all are symbolic representatives of what capitalism glories in and Odets systematically breaks the myths associated with them to suggest that they need to be replaced by others with a viable system. In the last episode, Agate explains the cliché-ridden allegation against the workers like "reds" and "Moscow Gold" meaning they get financial assistance from Russia. Meanwhile, the news reaches them that Lefty Costella, for whom they are waiting, will never arrive since he was found with a bullet in his head. Having read this, Agate comes out with a moving tirade which created a sensation in the thirties:

> HELLO AMERICA! HELLO WE'RE STORM-BIRDS OF THE WORKING-CLASS. WORKERS OF THE WORLD.. .. OUR BONES AND BLOOD. And when we die they'll know what we did to make a new world.[6]

And he asks the audience for the answer and the answer is: strike. The audience screams in unison with the characters on the stage The tremendous impact of the play is general and the ending in particular which is recounted by Harold Clurman, the architect of the Group Theatre, which is a Jewish group with a penchant for social drama:

> The first scene of the Lefty had not played two minutes when a shock of delighted recognition struck the audience like a tidal wave. Deep laughter, not assent, a kind of joyous fervour seemed to sweep the audience towards the stage. The actors no longer performed, they were being carried along as if by an exultancy of communication such as I had never witnessed in the theatre before... when the audience at the end of the play responded to the militant question for the stage . . . it was something more than a tribute to the play's effectiveness, more even than a testimony of the audience's hunger for constructive social action. It was the birth cry of the thirties.[7]

Odets did extensive journalistic work before he took up writing the play. In fact, Joseph North covered the New York strike for the *New Masses*. Odets personally met him and North described how in socialist countries like Russia racism is never found. Many references to racism especially anti-Semitism in Odet's play are intended to reflect the social prejudice of the times. And Communism of Russia appeared to be the only viable political ideology where every thing would be in the right place. The dialectical factor of alienation in capitalist countries is the major cause for the social dislocation. The small man is for ever battling against the hostile environment. The capitalist environment is a paradise for the exploiters and the small man is a perennial scapegoat in order to facilitate the animalistic urge of the rich. The conflict between man and environment and an essential stigma of alienation in the capitalist nations figures as an over-riding theme in many of his plays. But surprisingly enough, the Frankfurt School, which mostly consists of Jewish thinkers who, thanks to Nazism, became permanent emigres;, came up with a vigorous critique of bourgeois political institutions which not only give the lie to governmental success but also perpetuate the machinery of victimization without appearing to do so. Marcuse who is the father-figure of the American New Left movement has systematically demystified the capitalist ideal. It is so much in tune with the spirit of the times. Hence, plays like *Awake and Sing* (1935), *Paradise Lost* (1936), *The Big Knife* (1949) and *Golden Boy* (1947) continue to dramatize the agony of alienation. Although these plays deal with the people entrapped in circumstances, there are always few authorial voices which preach a radical solution. Jacob in *Awake and Sing* and Leo Gordon in *Paradise Lost* are such characters both subscribing to the radical vision which, they hope, can destroy the social malady. The liberal faith in individualism and the theory that man should be allowed to realize his own self, is brought under a critical examination. Ben Gordon, Joe Bonaparte and Charlie have their personal preferences but the tentacles of environment are irresistible. Consequently, they end up destroying their original talent and take up ascribed identities which, they feel, can provide a sense of solace. Once these different identities are achieved, they soon realize its futility since they had to sacrifice so much of their humanity. Another level of alienation sets in. Not equipped with moral courage and the sustaining value system to face such a crisis, they succumb to the ignominious solution in suicide. Much later in a response to the House of Un-American Activities Committee, Odets expresses his concern for man: "I see that one must do one of the two things: one must pick one's way very carefully through the maze of liberalism or leftism to-day or one must remain silent. Of the two I must tell you frankly I would try to pick the first way because the little I have to say, the little I have to contribute to the betterment or welfare of the American people could not permit me to be silent.''[8]

Critics never took kindly to him and in the luxury of post-Depression revisionism, he is categorically viewed as the playwright of the thirties. Although, this may be justified to a certain extent, the treatment given to the revival of his plays is uncalled for, if not biased. What happened to the romance with Soviet Communism is aptly summed up in Arthur Koestler's *Darkness at Noon* (1941), which was dramatized later by Sidney Kingsley. Whatever conclusions one could draw from the Moscow Trials which attained notoriety as Stalin Purges, there has been a tendency to rationalize Jewish radicalism in the thirties. While many trace the root to the religious scriptures, some critics identify Jewish messianism in Karl Marx. Thus socialism is Judaism secularized. The messianic age which establishes the kingdom of peace forever, has been faithfully assimilated in Marxism and given a secular interpretation. Arthur Liebman, who made a profound study of the Jews and the Left has this to say in this context:

> ... the most important aspect of Marx's teaching concerning the proletariat's messianic vocation is the fact that he applied to the proletariat the characteristics of God's chosen people. Marx was a Jew, he had abandoned the faith of his father, but the messianic expectation of Israel remained within his subconscious, and for him the proletariat is a new Israel, God's chosen people, the liberator and builder of an earthly kingdom that is to come. His proletarian Communism is a secularized form of the ancient Jewish chiliarm. A chosen class takes the place of the chosen people. It was impossible to reach such an idea by means of science. It is an idea of a religious kind. Here we have the very marrow of the communist religion. For messianic consciousness is surely always of ancient Hebrew origin.[9]

Rochelle Owen's *The Karl Marx Play* (1971) reflects this idea. Employing the techniques of the avant garde, she portrays Karl Marx as not only a genius but also as a poor father beset with pecuniary problems. To classify this play is a difficult task and the author herself calls it "tragedy/comedy" and "fantasy" with music. With the liberal use of language and songs in between, the play attempts to get into the essential spirit that moved Marx to write the *Manifesto*. Frequently Engels reminds him of being Jewish, though Marx says that he is a Prussian and an internationalist. Marx sees New Jerusalem—a messianic vision of peace and universal brotherhood. The New Jerusalem is obviously Marxian theory of proletarian dictatorship. The play has a typical Jewish family situation and gives the impression that Marx, schooled in adversity, takes revenge against the degradation in a philosophy which is to usher in a society where man is liberated from the external circumstances. Moved by personal misery and a stirring vision Marx says: "I scream unto you, the world is full of loathsome riff raff! Scum! Ought not a righteous dethroner of God! I damn you, grand father Yahveh! Yahveh! I am a righteous dethroner of God."[10] The relationship between the Hebrew Messianism and Marxism is connected convincingly by Owens.

Having made this point, it is worthwhile to turn to the works of Lillian Hellman who also wrote plays in the thirties but never accepted theatre as weapon. She doesn't take an ideological stance even in the radical decade. A liberal herself, she also could not turn her attention from the declining liberal values. In her autobiography, *Scoundrel Time,* which is about the Mc Carthy era, she writes:

> My belief in liberalism was mostly gone. I think I have substituted for it something private called, for want of something that should be more accurate, decency. And yet certain connecting strings have outworn many knives, perhaps because the liberal connections had been there for thirty years and that's a long time. There was nothing strange about the very problem, it is native to our time; but it is painful for a

native that can no longer accept liberalism not to be able to accept radicalism. One sits uncomfortably on a too comfortable cushion. Many of us now endlessly jump from one side to another and endlessly fall in space. The American creative world is not only equal but superior in talent to their colleagues in other countries, but they have given no leadership, written no words of new theory in a country that cries out for belief and, because it has none, find too many people acting in strange and aimless violence.[11]

However, this was written as a response to the "plague years" of the fifties when naming names was a fashionable virtue in order to save one's skin. But in the thirties and the forties, when Hellman's significant plays appeared, she was a strong liberal. Although her plays reflect her political views, there is also a streak of decline in the liberal spirit which only means that she is reflecting the mood of the times. She is even ambivalent at times as in *Days to Come*. It features a benevolent industrialist and equally honest workers on strike for their rights. The middlemen seize upon the crisis and take advantage of helpless situation. One never knows where Hellman's loyalties lie. Written in the thirties, the vision of the play is hazy, if not inconsistent.

Andrew Rodman has an amicable relationship with his workers. Once the workers are on strike, he does not know how to handle the situation, knowing that he does not have sound financial means to fulfil their demands. The family legal adviser takes over and immediately brings in the Wilkie boys, the gangsters, to run the factory with the help of some other workers brought from elsewhere. The union leader, Firth, wants to settle the crisis to their mutual benefit since Andrew has been a friend. Once the gangster force enters, they begin to work with subversive means. Whalen is a major force in the movement. Even Whalen comments that all the labour organizers are essentially racketeers but acknowledges that the situation is different in this factory. Workers like the boss,and the boss reciprocates their appreciation generously. In their words, there is a working relationship between them. Within no time, the strike-breakers plant a dead body at Whalen's place and the police are called. Firth's daughter is killed in the ensuing trouble. And the gap increases between the boss and the workers. Andrew himself faces a personal problem knowing that his wife is not faithful to him. At the end of the play, he orders the gangsters out from his house and realizes that it is no longer safe to move out. Here we have a businessman who is not an exploiter and the workers who have a cause. Only the mediators are villainous. The play's message is ambivalent in the sense that while creating a genial industrialist and genuine workers, the blame is shifted on to the mediators. But the question of the mediators exploiting the situation in itself, as the play suggests, is created by capitalist economy. One cannot break strikes without hurting someone. There is truth in Wilkie's comments:

> But I want to tell you, I've worked for a lot of men, some of them deacons of the Church who were breaking strikes for the good of America, but I never worked for a man before who believed I could come in, run his factory, and break his strike without walking on anybody's toes.[12]

Here is a peculiar situation for a writer of liberal convictions, writing a play for an audience in a time of extreme anti-liberal bias. Yet he is to solve the dilemma without belying his liberal views. Hence, Hellman takes up the same people—workers, industrialists and gangsters—and interprets them in order not to make disparaging comments on industrialists. In the process, both workers and industrialists are presented as good people and only the mediators are trouble-makers which is unconvincing especially when it is understandable that they are vehicles of Capitalist violence themselves. To make matters worse, the play takes a different line altogether by turning to Andrew's personal life. Hellman possibly knew that she could not find a solution to such an ambivalent treatment and hence concluded the play with a twist given to Andrew's life. Never did Hellman write a play about these themes again because, being a believing liberal, she found it difficult to rationalize her belief in the radical times and refute the spirit of the times. And yet, she takes the theme of liberal crisis by shifting to the decline of the west, which is a much safer ground. Nevertheless nowhere does the playwright give the impression that liberalism has lost its validity. On the other hand, she seems to imply that the rejection of the liberal temper would inevitably bring disaster to western civilization. The rise and prominence of totalitarianism in Germany and Fascist emergence in Italy substantiates this thesis. *Watch on the Rhine* (1940) is about Kurt Muller, a German refugee, who makes it a mission of his life to fight the Nazis. Hellman continues to present the aristocratic families of America. Kurt escapes to America only to face another set of problems in his mother-in-law's home who, despite her great family heritage, strongly supports his cause. Kurt has been a wanderer all along with his family. Part of an underground movement, he collects money from the poor farmers to support their movement. Having realized that Kurt does not have papers, Tech soon takes advantage of it. However, Kurt is familiar with these situations. Once understood that there is no end to Tech's blackmail, he kills Tech and continues his endless wanderings once again.

The breakdown of Europe is significantly shown in *The Searching Wind* (1944). The locale changes this time to all the centres of European civilization. Seen and interpreted from an American viewpoint, the play is a definitive study of the liberal crisis. The action takes place in Washington, Paris, Rome and Berlin. It also delves into the psyche of the young generation which has the moral responsibility, for the sake of humanity, to put all the splintered pieces of the West and rebuild a more humane civilization. They are not responsible for the disaster and yet they have the task of redeeming the situation.

The play opens with a spring evening in 1944 at ambassador Hazen's house. Moses Taney, a former newspaper man, reflects on the eventful, if sad, years he lived to see. His grandson, Sam Hazen, participated in the first world war in Rome at a time when his father was also there as embassy official. Yet, both have different views of the war. Alex, being an official, met more prominent people and probably only knew the governmental version of the war. Sam was in the army and he saw history taking shape for which he was not responsible in any way, though as an army man he was also taking part in it. Moses states that he had talks with Alex on many occasions about Victor Emmanuel the day when Mussolini marched into Rome. He watched Rome being taken over by the fascists. Then, he decided to give up his newspaper for good for he saw no hope for Europe. In the meantime, Ponette, the butler, recounts as to how his store had been taken away by radicals in Paris forcing him to the present state. But for the radicals, he surmises, the Germans would never have entered France. With these comments on the political scene, they move into the dining hall. The past is reenacted in the flashback style. First, the situation of Rome in 1922. Moses hears the sound of gun-firing outside his hotel. There are rumours that Mussolini will take over. The American embassy advises Moses not to make any statements since it may spoil their relationship with Italy. Later, he realized that Emmanuel invites Mussolini to take over. Moses knew the diplomatic justifications, one of them being that Mussolini would possibly destroy the forces of Communism in Italy. In the next part of the play, the Jewish persecution in Berlin is shown. In the Paris of 1938, a German diplomat tries to influence Alex when he is to send a report to America. The discussion touches Chamberlain's meeting with Hitler at the Munich Conference. The inevitable totalitarian presence, either in the form of Nazism or Fascism, in these centres of European culture questions Moses's liberal mind. His dilemma at the crossroads of history is painful especially when he knows that there is nothing sustaining that could become a useful substitute for liberal democracy. The last scene is once again the Hazen house. Sam tells his parents that his leg has to be amputated. He vehemently questions the stance taken by his parents and his grandfather as by-standers without making an attempt to change the course of history. He was proud of his parents until one day when his fellow-army man gives a newspaper clipping which says that many of the self-proclaimed righteous people had business dealings with Germany.

The play seems to suggest that Sam Hazen is an unwilling participant in history, while the people who are responsible for the situation quietly make their decisions in the convenient corridors of power. Moses; cries at the news that Sam will be amputated. But he is a helpless liberal himself and he sees the destruction of his personal convictions. Hellman's treatment of the liberal crisis is interesting since despite many setbacks, she never questions the validity of her liberal views. The liberal characters remain as shattered people. It should also be noted that these political themes become useful background material often becoming the major thematic preoccupation. But Hellman also creates other personal situations to make it more effective. Though her plays point to certain social circumstances of a particular stage in history, the universal situations make her plays timeless in their treatment of the human predicament. Hellman knew that the themes with a more than excessive emphasis on social factors of a particular period sometimes bordering on didacticism could easily make her plays obsolete as it happened with many writers of the thirties though some of them deserved better. The only way to solve this problem is to create situations of universal importance with a strong background of the social structure of the times which is not only verbal in their explicit political views but also prominent in their social inferences. This is precisely the reason why her plays are produced with affirmative critical appreciation while many of the committed and left oriented playwrights of the thirties, with few exceptions like Odets, are rarely produced.

Arthur Miller, more than any other dramatist, wrote a powerful play on the fifties against Mc Carthy's congressional committee which made a mockery of the liberal concepts like individualism and freedom. The only other writer to attempt a powerful critique of Mc Carthy era is E.L. Doctorow who in *The Book of Daniel* tells the ignominy of Joe Mc Carthy's Congressional Committees and what they symbolize in terms of the liberal crisis. Miller is a major playwright who explored the liberal dilemma in post-war Europe. He explains his theoretical views in his works:

> In all my plays and books I try to take settings and dramatic situations from life which involve real questions of right and wrong. Then I set out, rather implacably and in the most realistic situations I can find, the moral dilemma and try to point a real, though hard, path out. I don't see how you can write anything decent without using the question of right and wrong as basis.[13]

That his plays emphasize the ethical and moral perspective is unquestionable. The ethical rationale for the witch-hunt of the fifties is investigated in *The Crucible* (1952). The fifties is the decade of betrayals and "naming names." The radical intellectuals who suffered an emotional tragedy in the late thirties were to face another nightmare before the HUAC who took the role of the Grand Inquisitors. For once, the democratic ideals seemed to be on the brink of collapse. Once the fallacy of Stalin's Communism was known in America in the late thirties, the intellectuals began to reassess their stance. Also, the war relieved the pains of the Great Depression. And there were a number of plays once again affirming Americanism. Kaufman and Hart wrote *The American Way* (1939) and Robert E. Sherwood's patriotic drama *Abe Lincoln in Illinois* (1938) not only told the story of Lincoln's life, but it also warned Americans of the perpetual danger to totalitarianism. The upsurge of the American spirit could hardly tolerate the radical vision. Determined to see the threat from Communism and Fascism, the Americans approved the congressional committees which put the radicals on trial. The governments and especially Joseph Mc Carthy The littlemen in Salem become easy prey to the theocratic establishment though Proctor and even Francis knew that it was a hoax. Even Mary Warren whom Proctor takes to the court, could not resist the mass hysteria and immediately becomes a victim to Abigail's talk of flying yellow eagle and impulsively calls Proctor a man of the devil. Unable to tolerate the hoax which is being legalized, Proctor tears the government order. When his wife is implicated Proctor says:

> Why do you never wonder if Parris be innocent, or Abigail? Is the accurser holy now? Were they born this morning as clean as God's fingers? I will tell you what's walking Salem—Vengeance is walking Salem. We are what we always were in Salem, but now the little crazy children are jangling the keys of the kingdom, and common vengeance writes the law.[14]

When it is a matter of life and death, Proctor decides to sign the confession. But he refuses to give the letter of Danforth. With a helpless cry of his soul, he wonders how he can live without the sanctity of his name. He refuses to give the letter of confession with his name on it "because I cannot have another in my life! Because I lie and sign myself to lies."[15] And finally he gets prepared for his fate and the new sun shines on Elizabeth's face, symbolic of newly regained dignity in the face of temptation from every side to be otherwise.

Miller makes effective use of history in order to draw lessons for contemporary American society. The play itself received mixed reviews, getting rave reviews when it was revived in the sixties. On the first production, his own acquaintances avoided him for it was presented at the height of the Mc Carthy period. The play attacks the myth of sanctimonious government which acts as an arbiter of ethical values and forces the audience to draw useful inferences. One wonders if the long cherished values of individualism and freedom are not distorted owing to the excessive participation of government in the individual lives to the extent of determining how one should think and act. The theme of betrayal is repeated in *After the Fall* (1964) when the victim of the witch-hunt commits suicide. Miller himself comments:

> In the countries of the Communist ideology, all resistance of any import is linked to the totally malign capitalist succubi, and in America any man who is not reactionary in his views is open to the charge of alliance with Red hell.[16]

Together, then, the three playwrights investigate the liberal dilemma though with different angles of creative vision. Odets, the product and the spokesman of the thirties, truly voiced the feelings of his generation. The radical intellectuals comfortably believed that the disaster brought in by the liberal capitalism can only be redeemed by Communism. Richard Crossman is right when he says:

> The intellectual attraction of Marxism was that it exploited the liberal fallacies which really were fallacies. It taught the bitter truths that progress is not automatic, that boom and slump are inherent in capitalism, that social injustice and racial discrimination are not cured merely by the passage of time. . . . Western democracy today is not so callous or so materialistic as it was in that dreary armistice between the wars. But it has taken two world wars and two totalitarian revolutions to make it begin to understand that its task is not to allow progress to do its work for it but to provide an alternative to world revolution by planning the co-operation of free people.[17]

However the writers in the thirties are only critical about the American disaster and never have they applied, as Daniel Aaron suggests,[18] the same sense of evaluation in assessing the situation in Russia after the October Revolution which, not surprisingly, became a source of disenchantment later. Unlike Odets who certainly believed that the liberal temper is out of step with times, Hellman and Miller continued to have faith in it. Despite the fact that they dramatized the ugly reality of the liberal crisis, they never totally rejected it. In fact, they seem to suggest since liberal democracies were ruined, Western civilization had reached a point of human degradation which resulted in the emergence of totalitarian philosophy.

In retrospect, these playwrights undoubtedly share their concern for the common man who is pushed to the periphery of turbulent history. Odets felt that it is the common man who was always sacrificed for the welfare of a few capitalists who were responsible for the social dislocation. His commitment to the common man made him realize that, only he absence of capitalism could save man from his perennial alienation. Russian Communism, which not only provides common necessities but also believes in the proletarian dictatorship, convinced his deeply felt humanism. And his plays stand as a testimony to his supreme faith in humanity. Neither Hellman nor Miller had this problem, though they showed their concern about the decline of liberal institutions. If the danger is from the external forces of Fascism in Hellman's plays, Miller writes about the danger within—Mc Carthy's plague years. Both of them are aware that it is individualism which is attacked and destroyed for the apotheosis of abstract regimentation. Taken to the extreme point, Hellman sensed, these forces could annihilate what is dear to human dignity and the spirit of tolerance. Miller, on his part, sensed ruthlessness and danger in the arbitrary judgmental tone, adopted by Mc Carthy during the witch-hunt era. And the degeneration and willing participation of people in the work of the committee is sharply criticised in his plays. The moral and ethical questions raised in the plays are pertinent and show his commitment to the freedom of human choice. To sum up, these writers reflected their commitment to human dignity. Their plays also reflect the horrendous journey that liberal philosophy had to survive and somehow continue to exist in different possible ways.

NOTES

1. Max Sevell, *Is Liberalism Dead?* (Seattle: University of Washington Press, 1967), p. 3.
2. R. Cohen Morris, *Faith of a Liberal* (New York: Henry Holt, 1946). While considering spinoza as a liberal prophet who rejected anthropomorphic God, he states that it sprang from anthropomorphism. In the same book he also discusses Zionism wondering if it is liberalism or tribalism. Written much before the Holocaust, the original essay attacks Zionism for its exclusiveness. In the present collec-

tion, he writes a note which is a revision of his ideas, stating that just as perverted deeds can be done by a good philosophy, good things also can be done by a false creed.

3. Leo Strauss, *Liberalism: Ancient and Modern* (New York: Basic Books, 1968). He discusses *The Guide* in terms of liberal tradition. It underlines a sense of liberation in its interpretation of the Holy Scriptures.
4. Gottfried Lessing, *Nathan the Wise* (New York: Leypoldt and Holt, 1868). The play is an example of the Age of Reason. Lessing looks at the Jewish question and rationalizes as to why Jews are the way they are. He feels that their conditions are the reason for their present state. A believer in naturalist school, never does he question the stereotypical myth, but looks for rationalization in environmental determinism. And the solution he suggests is to take the Jews away from these circumstances. Though a questionable premise, it still can be called an attempt at liberal attitude towards the centuries of prejudices.
5. Clifford Odets, *Till the Day I Die, Six Plays* (New York: Random House, 1939), p. 159.
6. Clifford Odets, *Waiting for Lefty, Six Plays*, p. 31
7. Harold Clurman, *The Fervent Years* (New York: Harcourt Brace, 1945, 1975), pp. 147-48.
8. Clifford Odets, *Thirty Years of Treason*, ed. Eric Bentley (New York: The Viking Press, 1971), p. 531.
9. Arthur Liebman, *Jews and the Left* (New York: Wiley, 1979).
10. Rochelle Owens, *The Karl Marx Play, Best Short Plays of 1971* (Radnor, Pa: Chilton Book Company, 1971), p. 233.
11. Lillian Hellman, *The Scoundrel Time, Three* (Boston: Little, Brown and Company, 1979), p. 679
12. Lillian Hellman, *Days to Come, The Collected Plays* (Boston: Little, 1961, 1971), p. 124.
13. Arthur Miller, *The Theatre Essays of Arthur Miller*, ed. Robert A. Martin (New York: Viking Press, 1978), p. XVII.
14. Arthur Miller, *The Crucible, Collected Plays* (New York: Viking Press, 1957), p. 281.
15. *Ibid.*, p. 328.
16. *Ibid.*, p. 249.
17. Richard Crossman, *The God That Failed* (New York: Harper and Row, 1944, 1945), p. 5.
18. Daniel Aaron, *Writers on the Left* (New York: Harcourt Brace

World, 1961). In this definitive book on the journey of the left and the social basis that ultimately led them to Communism, Aaron builds up the actuality of certain incidents that eventually turned out to be perennial metaphors of capitalist exploitation. The trials of Scottsboro boys and the execution of Sacco and Vanzetti moved the creative imagination. The declining social order and the Wall Street crash precipitated their disenchantment. The John Reed Clubs, Michael Gold, *New Masses* became inevitable symbols of the "red" decade. In retrospect, it may appear that the writers were over-enthusiastic and failed to see the horror in Russia which was brewing and which came to be known as Moscow Trials.

Crimes against Humanity: Holocaust, War and the Jew

In one of his parables, Franz Kafka writes about a man from the country who seeks admittance to the Law. The doorkeeper initially objects stating that it is not possible at the moment. So, the man from the country waits. In the process, some kind of indifferent conversation follows with the doorkeeper. The man on his part gives him whatever he has as a bribe for admittance. The doorkeeper takes it only to give the impression that the other man has tried in every possible way. As it happens, he is not the only doorkeeper, there are three more and each one is more awful in appearance than the others. Time passes and the Law-seeker gets old. As a final gesture, he summons up his energy and asks the doorkeeper a question before his death: "Every one strives to reach the Law . . . so how does it happen that for all these many years no one but myself has ever begged for admittance?"[1]

Having realized that the man has reached his end the door-keeper tells him that no one can be admitted here since it is meant for him and then he starts to close it permanently.

In this parable, Kafka attempts to probe into the heart of darkness of modern times and the minimal self of modern man. The Law-seeker never gets to reach it and spends his life in the hope of getting to it. The reasons for his failure one never knows. Kafka, in his inimitable style, does not give even a hint. When the man asks the only question, the door man tells him that this door is meant for him and for none other. Does it mean that every seeker has its own Law that ends up in unremitting quest? The parable, however, makes one point clear: Man and the Law are for ever isolated. It is the quintessential Kafkaesque vision which captures the decadence of the times, together with the reductive stature of man. His parables significantly establish themselves as the archetypal modes of the modern experience that are to become more compelling in terms of an obnoxious stage that man has reached; and more immediate because Kafka's vision foretells the ruthless limits to which the Enlightenment has been taken only to result in the tyranny of the primacy of the rational self or intellect. The parable is paradigmatic of modern man's need to have the spiritual ambience that can bless his life with some kind of meaning and the fact that one cannot achieve such a state of unity. Each man struggles with the consciousness of inner void and looks desperately for the redeeming structure of life enriching unity only to realize its futility. It also foretells the doom that now haunts the post-Holocaust generation. The irrational and the absurd therefore become the literary motif of the twentieth century creative vision which can be explained within the context of Kafka's parable. This should also serve as a starting point for Holocaust literature. Rosenfeld, while writing about the contemporary atmosphere of culture sums up what he calls "an age of enormity":

> Unfortunately there is nothing else into which we can fit our experience—traditions are broken and culture is unavailable. Our culture is an empty form, standing for a continuity of experience which is now discontinued, for the reality and inviolability of human values that are everywhere violated and denied. . . . Today the cultured man is isolated . . . the cultural form that conveyed humanity and assured the transaction from one man to the next has been destroyed.[2]

Rosenfeld, thus, emphasizes the realm of barbarity and points out the predicament a writer encounters in the absence of such a situation which could have facilitated the "transaction" between the writer and the reader. With this background in view, the inhumanity and horror of the Holocaust and the plight of a writer who has to struggle for strategies of "transaction" in order to convey his perception of evil to the reader, can be analyzed. This, in fact, brings us back to Franz Kafka who did not live to see the

Holocaust as such but, in more ways than one, had anticipated the subversion of humanity in his parables, stories, and novels. To communicate the heart of darkness, he adopts the techniques of farce, fantasy and absurdity in his evocative prose which certainly guided the latter-day *avant-garde* literature. The writers of the Holocaust, more important, the Holocaust dramatists, found his techniques useful and successfully employed them to advantage which is otherwise impossible. This does not necessarily suggest that they are always successful at it, since the Holocaust throws an essential burden, which is as moralistic as it is ethical, on the creative writer. Elie Wiesel, while commenting on the questions raised by the Holocaust literature, emphatically argues: "One generation later, it can still be said and must now be affirmed. There is no such thing as a literature of the Holocaust, nor can there be. The very expression is a contradiction in terms. Auschwitz negates any form of literature, as it defies all systems, all doctrines. . . . A novel about Auschwitz is not a novel, or else it is not about Auschwitz. The very attempt to write such a novel is blasphemy."[3] Wiesel is not the first to say this; and certainly many critics and survivors conform to this view. T.W. Adorno 's view, that writing poetry after Auschwitz is barbaric, became an acceptable dictum. But the fact remains that creative writers did try to grapple with this problem, for, how can a creative writer avoid the Planet Auschwitz? And, on the other hand, how can he communicate the horror of the death-camp to the reader? In spite of these exigencies, some writers tried to face the challenge. The Holocaust writers, then, are divided into three categories: the survivor who writes about the Holocaust; the creative writer who was never there and yet visualizes it and translates his vision into creative writing; and, the gentile writer who tries to get into the essence of the horror and gives his own interpretation. All of them have a moral responsibility of creating the structure of imagination in order to communicate it to the reader. The reader or the audience, in the case of drama, has a responsibility of familiarizing himself with the history to participate in the creative expression. With regard to the survivors, they have to reach into their memory and sort out the reality, put it into an organized system and look for the strategies of communication. These are the inevitable problems and any failure can give the lie to the horror the death camps perpetuated, which is why so many Jewish critics and survivors protested against Holocaust literature. But then, Wiesel himself wrote stories and novels and retold the stories of the Hasidic masters, which also proves that however difficult and insurmountable the task may be, one has to make an attempt to tell it, lest posterity forget that there was one such realm of experience called the Holocaust. Although it is a challenge to the literary imagination, the writer should be conscious of the perils of such an act. Langer's views, in this connection, are pertinent:

> How should art—how can art?—represent the inexpressibly inhuman suffering of the victims, without doing an injustice to that suffering? If art, as Adorno concedes, is perhaps the last remaining sanctuary where the suffering can be paid honest homage, enshrining it permanently in the imagination of the living as the essential horror that it was, the danger also exists of this noble intention sliding into abyss of its opposite.[4]

The Theatre with the multiple channels of communication and multiplicity of techniques that can profitably be used to tackle enigmatic realities, is undoubtedly an effective medium for the Holocaust writers, though their achievement is debatable on many levels. The successful playwrights did make use of *avant garde* techniques to unravel the mystery of evil, while some used the straightforward well-made play structure, for their tale needed such a method.

In the following pages, the plays which reflect responses to the Holocaust either remotely or directly, are discussed on three levels. Setting the tone of the argument with *The Deputy* (1964) and *The Man in the Glass Booth* (1968), the two significant plays that raise the fundamental questions, an attempt has been made to consider the plays where the World War and the Jewish problem are of topical interest. Finally, the plays where the Holocaust becomes the central subject matter are analyzed. Rolf Hochhuth's *The Deputy* (1964) deals with Papal indifference to the mass killings in Hitler's Germany at a time when Papal intervention would have made a difference. The play created a controversy ever since its first production. Some critics like Albert von Kessel defended the Pope. Had the Pope come up with any statement against Hitler, he would have been killed and later Hitler would have announced that the Pope was killed when trying to escape, reasoned Albert von Kessel. Whatever may be the rationale for such a defence, it would be impossible to underscore the moral aspect the play unquestionably touches upon. The Pope, the deputy of Jesus Christ, should have protested against the savage behaviour of the totalitarian regime since not doing so undermines the credibility of Catholic doctrine. In five acts, the play is about Father Ricardo who struggles in vain to convince Papal authorities to denounce Hitler's Germany. The play starts with a conversation between Ricardo and the Nuncio. The Nuncio's argument is that only baptized Jews would come under his scope. Gerstein, who is forced to be a Nazi officer, asks the Nuncio to tear the Concordat executed by the Pope and Hitler. In the next scene, Adolf Eichman appears and the doctors inform him that they have been experimenting on Jewish skulls. There are some conscientious people among the Nazis like Gerstein and the doctor. Gerstein makes a strong impression on Ricardo who tells him that even the priests are praying for Hitler. The doctor's words that it is a contradiction to have a good mind and remain a Christian would spell out the dilemma a believer seems to face. The history is revealed slowly in the first act. The nuns with Jewish blood are turned over to the Nazis in Holland; though many Germans saved Jews at the risk of their lives. The second act takes us to Rome. Ricardo has a discussion with his father, Fontana. Fontana expresses the Pope's intention that only Hitler could save Europe from the Russians and unite the west. The Pope also calls Roosevelt's demand for Hitler's unconditional support "un-Christian." The Cardinal, in turn, generalizes that the minorities always have to face such crises and that the Jews overdrew on "the credit they had been given/there in Germany." (262) While these responses are expressly used to rationalize the Pope's non-intervention, Ricardo's comments that the Christians are always linked with the people Jesus belonged to, are emphatic. His deep-seated agony is expressed in his words to his father: "Let us admit at last: these flames are also our trial by fire!/Who will, in times to come, respect us still/ as moral arbiters, if, in this time,/we fail so miserably."[5]

After eight months duration, the Pope has done nothing which is the reason for severe arguments among Gerstein, Ricardo, and the Cardinal. The Papal policy strongly believes in the theory that Hitler is the only decisive force that can destroy the Russians. Gerstein explains the fallacy of Russian supremacy which is a myth propagated by, first, Napoleon and, later, by Bismarck, Frederick and Willhelm the Second. Hitler is taking advantage of the myth planted in the minds of Germans. Gerstein, repelled by the Cardinal's words, states:

> If God
> did not desire us to perish, why would He
> strike us Christians with such fearful blindness?
> For sixteen months now Rome has known
> of Hitler's savage butcheries in Poland
> Why not a word about it from the Pope-
> that where on Sundays the church bells ring,
> on weekdays the flesh of men is burned
> That is the Christian West to-day
> Why, Your Eminence, should not God
> send us a new deluge?
> Only Stalin's tanks can liberate
> Auschwitz, Treblinka, Maidenik. . . .[6]

A few minutes later, Ricardo says that if the doctor or the businessman or the working man can risk his life by giving asylum, the silence of the Pope has no justification. In the absence of Papal protest, Ricardo decides to go with the prisoners who are driven to the gas chambers, with the hope that at least his gesture would save the concept of the Papacy. Ricardo sees no sustaining logic in the

Papal belief that Hitler would save Europe. Gerstein, in fact, suggests that if someone could announce from the Papal radio that the Pope denounces the killings, the situation may be relieved a little. The efforts of persuasion continue. This time it is Ricardo's father, Fontana; he does not mention even the word Jew specifically even after the fact that some Jews are taken away from Rome. In the meantime, Ricardo also tries to convince the Pope. Having realized the futility, Ricardo says: "God shall not destroy His Church/ only because a Pope shrinks from His summons."[7]

Ricardo goes with the other prisoners of the camp. Gerstein wants to help him out but Ricardo refuses and asks Jacobson, instead, to go which also fails. With the background of the camps, a loudspeaker voice states the historical truth that the Pope never made any denouncements against Hitler. At the end we see a dead body of a Jewess and the loudspeaker concludes that Hitler finally orders the camps to be blown up as the war comes to an end.

A sad commentary on the religious institutions which supposedly guard the ethical dimension of man's life and yet fail to respond when the testing time stands before them only because of certain political justifications, not based on reality but on the inherited vague myths. Extensive research was undertaken for this play which gives moral strength to the central theme.

Robert Shaw's *The Man in the Glass Booth* delves into the psyche of a survivor and how he faces reality after the war. The survivor has the burden of guilt of his survival when many are gassed to death, which questions the rationale of his survival. Also, his realization that the world can never understand the perversity of the mass killings forces him to look for strategies to use them as useful means of communication. Although it is not as effective as *The Deputy*, it focusses on a different aspect by presenting the dilemma of a survivor, Colonel Dorff, an SS officer. When the play opens, we see Goldman in his New York apartment, a flourishing businessman and philanthropist and yet living a single life. On his fifty-second birthday, he realizes that the Pope had at last pardoned the Jews and he also feels that some people are following him. True enough the Israeli intelligence spots him and forces him to come with them under the impression that he is the SS officer Dorff. In Israel, he is put on trial. Mrs. Reisen, an Israeli secret police official, does not understand why he chose to live like a Jew. However, after intense arguments in the court, Goldman plays the role of the Colonel Dorff giving the gory details of his killings. In the meantime, an old woman from the audience announces that he is not Adolf Karl Dorff but a German Jew. She also explains the strange episode about the SS officer who used to be friendly with Goldman probably because of his resemblance with him. The reason for Goldman's behaviour, Mrs. Reisen thinks, is that he is a self-hating Jew. Later he grafted the camp number and put on the SS insignia to pass off as a Nazi officer. He possibly inveigled some Israeli Intelligence officer into believing that he is the dreaded criminal who has to be put on trial for the knowledge of the civilized world. Goldman tells the court what happened after the liberation. He practised the barbarity of the Russian cossacks and "rode on Russian horses and we battered Polish castles, we looted museums, we broke, we burned, we raped and we drank."[8] Having spoken these words, he goes into the glass booth and locks himself up and then the lights fade. The play focusses on the survivor's knowledge of savagery and his response to it. Liberated from the camps, he wanted to live the life of the oppressor and do what they did to the Jews. Although it is an extreme version of a survivor, it also shows the tragic side of a man who has seen so much and tolerated so much as to make it difficult for him to grapple with the world where the people live normal lives because he would never belong there. The Pope's belated pardon of the Jews, his masochistic tendencies and his ultimate role, though personal, will speak the truth of the human perversity which caused him so much anguish. The guilt, the life to be lived and the perennial moral questions become a menace to his sanity. His traumatic life is a true testimony to the barbarity of the camps which distorted reality and its suggestiveness of the place for all eternity.

Peter Weiss's *The Investigation* (1966) is a lengthy play which tells the story of the disaster of the War. Not essentially a Jewish point of view, it encompasses the story of the War from various angles. Hence, we see the accused Nazi officials and the surviving witnesses giving their different versions. He builds the momentum of his theme of investigation in a series of scenes called the songs of the platform, the camp, the possibility of survival, the death of Lili Tofler, S.S.Corporal Stark, the black wall, phenol, the bunker block, cyclone B. and the fire ovens. In the process, each of them becomes a metaphor of human savagery. Although the play can be appreciated for its attempt at a historical view, it may also have to face criticism for making it impersonal and thus underscoring the trial of humanity. In the prolonged discussions, the audience is informed of the details from start to finish by both parties. The play ends with the comments of the accused who feels that it is time to forget the past which the other accused applaud. However, the play is significant in that it also presents the non-Jewish angle to the War. Together, these European plays bring out three different perspectives. While the first two can be credited with the emphasis on the moral side of man, Peter Weiss's attempt at historical assessment can create more problems than it purportedly tries to solve.

The American writer's response to the Holocaust is a story in itself. The writer who wrote about it never had first-hand knowledge. This, at least, partly speaks for the failure of first-rate works on the Holocaust, not to ignore the mediocrity of its imaginative representation in the form of marginal characters of the Holocaust. Before taking those few plays which face the tyranny that the Holocaust imposes on the creative writer, the plays where the Holocaust is merely a reference are summed up for whatever inferences that can be drawn from them. Similarly, there are certain plays of the World War in which the Jewish experience takes on different perspectives. The American writer of the Holocaust has to rely on available history to bring veracity to his tale. Even if he has a thorough knowledge of the events, presenting them in a convincing manner through his artistic vision is not a small task. The necessity of ethical and moral perspective, without which the creative interpretation of the Holocaust is meaningless, forces the writer to enter into another realm of difficulties, for, to establish such a pattern of ethical dimension, he has to accommodate history by providing a suitable human situation. All these efforts may not necessarily guarantee success on both moral and literary levels. On the other hand, his failure may cause a distorted understanding of the Holocaust which is a disservice to human suffering. The American writer is probably aware of these problems. Consequently, few works of literary excellence have come out from them. Edward Lewis Wallant's *The Pawn Broker* is more effective than Saul Bellow's *Mr Sammler's Planet*, for, it tries to grapple with the survivor's psyche and the trauma that is created by such a realm of experience—the camp's inhumanity and post-war security. John Hersy's *The Wall* tells the story of a fictional hero who supposedly leaves his diary so that posterity would know the way it was in Poland. None of them lives upto the achievement of writers like Elie Wiesel, Paul Celan, and Nelly Sachs who in their different ways successfully depict the horror.

However, the American playwright is not indifferent to the reality and is content to project anti-Semitism, or more specifically, to concentrate on the image of the Jew in the period of the War. As a result, the crisis of the Jew is treated with a singular devotion. The Jew also becomes the universal paradigm for the inhumanity of man to man. The absurdity, the irrationality, the existential angst and the *avant-garde* ethos are identified or interpreted through the image of the Jew. The theme of anti-Semitism figures prominently in the drama of the late thirties. Clifford Odets, S.N. Behrman, Lillian Hellman, and Sidney Kingsley, and others, have touched upon this theme. Kaufman and Hart's *The American Way* goes a little further in the glorification of American democracy and builds a rhetoric in its favour against the totalitarian mania for the racial theories. Being Jewish, they are aware of the plight of the Jew and hence have believed that only in the liberal democracies the idea of racism could be destroyed. Arthur Laurents's *Home of the Brave* deals with the psychological trauma that anti-Semitism imposes on the young mind of Coney. Coney, an American Jew, is one of the soldiers at a Pacific Base to fight against the Japanese forces. When the play begins, he is found in the hospital. Dr. Bilterger recognizes his problem and tries to make Coney recollect the entire situation.

Owing to a psychological setback, he cannot walk and the doctor, in order to know the actual event so that he can make Coney realize that he has no reason to feel guilty, forces him to narrate what had happened. Coney and Finch are friends and the latter even thinks in terms of arranging a marriage between his sister and Coney. T.J. always makes comments against Coney, calling Jews "kikes" and "sheenies." When Coney realizes that even Finch is no exception to the general anti-Semitism, he experiences a nervous shock. Consequently, it makes him happy when Finch is shot by the enemies. Later, Coney is forced to go with the soldiers leaving Finch behind since the maps have to be given to the authorities which finally foil the planned attacks of the enemies. However, Coney feels that the fact that he has left behind Finch proves that he is no different from the gentiles. This guilt-feeling is fixed in his mind. He cannot walk any more owing to this guilt-fixation. The doctor ultimately succeeds in proving that anybody, even a Jew, feels the same way at the time of war. This is practically proved when Mingo tells him that when a soldier was shot, he felt relieved that it was not him. This incident finally brings Coney back to the realization that the anti-Semitic comments of some soldiers are baseless. Arthur Laurents knew about the persecution of Jews. By 1946, the year of the play's publication, the story of the death camps is known to the civilized world. That he makes an attempt to evaluate the impact of prejudices on the young minds instead of handling the theme of the Holocaust, may be explained in terms of the difficulties such an effort involves. The displacement caused by the War is depicted in S.N. Behrman's *Jacobowsky and the Colonel* and Elmer Rice's *Flight to the West* (1940). While Behrman's play is about homeless Jocobowsky in Nazi-infested Paris, *Flight to the West* provides a platform for the political discussion as to what form of political ideology can be humane. Jacobowsky is a schlemiel-figure aware of the agony of the wandering Jew but danger. Changing places, he carries his portable exile pining to plant his roots in vain. He gains the admiration of the fleeing Polish Colonel and others; he is also ready to sacrifice even his life for others. The Polish Colonel's comments that he cannot leave Jacobowsky behind because he has no place now affirms the commitment of a civilized man to essential humanity. On the other hand, the fleeing Jews in *Flight to the West* are bedevilled by a shattered faith. When the discussion follows the argument whether Jews should have children, Frau Rosenthal vehemently rejects the idea on the premise that the world is no longer safe for Jewish children. The entire action takes place in the transatlantic aircraft flying to the west—a symbolic assertion that only the liberal west can save humanity from damnation. The aircraft seems to have members of all political persuasions: a Nazi, a Russian, and a liberal. In a long discussion, the liberal Ingraham accepts that his liberalism failed miserably in not rising to the occasion. However, the play suggests that it is only the west that can sustain a hope for the suffering humanity. Further, Elmer Rice is evidently concerned about the Jewish persecution. The Zionist implications are suggested in the character of Frau Rosenthal. In Dore Schary's *The Devil's Advocate* (1961), which is an adaptation of the Morris West novel, Aldo Meyer is presented as a humanist committed to the welfare of mankind. However, the shadow of the Nazi forces continues to spread its tentacles. Not a believer in any religion, he nevertheless sticks to his Jewishness. A respected doctor in an Italian village, he feels that he could not win the hearts of the people despite his service to the village. His life is strangely associated with Giacomo Nerone, a deserter who is worshipped by the people after his death. Dr. Aldo Meyer is a Jew seeking refuge and his portrayal deserves appreciation, for the priest, who plays the role as *advocatus diaboli*, and others show enormous respect for his commitment to the welfare of the villagers. He emerges as a man of humanistic convictions, though he knew that German forces could ship him to the concentration camps, the moment they knew about his existence. When Blaise Meredith comes to investigate the matter whether Nerone is a saintly person, he serves as the doctor for the ailing priest. Here religious tolerance between Catholicism and Judaism is suggested, though Dr. Meyer is a non-believing Jew. Joseph Heller, in *Claringer's Trial* and *We Bombed in New Haven*, continues to explore his favourite themes: black humour and the absurdity of contemporary life. His treatment of anti-Semitism and the irrationality of the War ultimately conforms to the absurd vision he seems to find in contemporary America. Lanford Wilson's *Talley's Folly* (1969) is a romantic comedy. The Jewish past of Matt Friedman is only marginal. These American plays portray the image of a Jew during the World War. Sometimes the Jewishness is marginal, and when it appears prominent, these plays are content in projecting the stigma of anti-Semitism. These plays could effectively bring out the inexpressible agony of the persecuted Jew. Ronald Ribman's *Cold Storage* (1977) is yet another example of the marginal treatment of the Jewish problem, though it successfully externalizes the agony of Richard Landau, a survivor, who lost his family in the camps. Having come to the cancer hospital for a check-up, he comes in contact with Parmigian who keeps asking him about Jewish secrets and the Kabbala. With grim humour, the play appears to be an exorcism for Parmigian and Landau who, in their different ways, come to terms with life. For Landau realizes, in the process of an educative conversation with the sometimes-irritating Parmigian, that his survival does not have to make him feel guilty. Landau says that he is "tired of being a man."[9] He is ambivalent about God's indifference which haunts him, for, he thinks that God killed his every link with the past. Landau saw the price one has to pay for survival. His father doing dishes in many restaurants for the sake of mere survival, troubles him. And God's absence when every shred of human dignity is abandoned makes them review the whole situation: "You die in concentration camp and His hand reaches into your mouth for the gold teeth and you know him. A handcuff falls off your wrist and you think you can escape until his fingers snap shut again, and you know Him."[10] Parmigian reminds him that there is no God but only men who should be responsible for one another and preserve their humanity. That Landau suffers from guilt for his survival and the failure of the divine presence in a particular time of history, makes him live the life of a non-participant in the here and now, which Parmigian promptly points out stating that Landau never got out of the police station where he was detained. The horror still haunts him. He reminds Landau of the reality that he is still waiting for the judges to give a verdict when they, as well as the victims, died long ago. In other words, he is looking for the impossibility instead of facing up to the facts. And suddenly, at this juncture, Landau remembers the name of a person at the police station who desperately was trying to find means to escape which, symbolically, acts as the only indication that Landau may come to terms with the present instead of living in the past. On his part, Parmigian knows that what Landau lived through is worse than a tragedy. It was monumental and compared to what happened to him, "Oedipus putting out his eyes was a minor occurrence."[11] Nevertheless, one cannot live with the monument; and the real suffering "is a catastrophe without a language." (339) Having said that, he still argues with Landau that he also should live in the present which initially appears to Landau as an act of absurdity. The play ends with Landau wheeling Parmigian inside and Parmigian promising him an interesting story the next day.

The significance of the play lies in the fact that it tries to present the psyche of the survivor and the enormous loss that does not give him a moment of respite. The major discussion about Landau occurs in the last few moments of the play, the overriding theme being the two cancer patients viewing life from different angles and facing the foreknowledge of death.

Barney Greenwald, in Herman Wouk's *The Caine Mutiny Court-Martial* (1954), is not a survivor but his knowledge of the Nazi crimes is so compunctious that he is determined to turn the court-martial of Steve Maryk into a personal battle against Tom Keeper. Greenwald takes up the case of Maryk, since he knew that it is Tom Keeper who fed Maryk with psychological terms. Maryk is court-martialled because he relieved his commander Capt. Queeg with no available evidence of his paranoia or irresponsibility. Greenwald's analysis is that Maryk, on his own, would not have dared to take up such a step. It is Tom Keeper who built up a negative opinion on Capt. Queeg, explained the terms like paranoia and neurosis, and finally told him that Maryk's medical log on Capt. Queeg proves that he is a paranoid—all this at a time when people like Capt. Queeg should be fighting against the Nazis. Greenwald realizes that it is Keeper's instigation that eventually stopped the ship from functioning. Even so, Keeper is not directly involved and hence Maryk is the scapegoat. Greenwald's only strategy is to spoil the case of Capt. Queeg and prove that he, at that moment, showed signs of paranoia. This logic could bring acquittal for Maryk. Greenwald cleverly elicits the signs of paranoia from a psychiatrist and the cases of Capt. Queeg's questionable conduct from other witnesses. When Capt. Queeg is asked to give his version of Maryk's medical log, he falls into the trap of this strategy. Later, Maryk's authenticated fitness certificate given by him, is presented to the court which decisively provides a chance for Maryk's acquittal.

However, Greenwald feels sorry to argue against Capt. Queeg, though it is inevitable in order to get at Tom Keeper. He remarks that he has to do this much against his will, for, it is the people like Capt. Queeg who stopped the Nazis from the possibility of occupying America, in which case his mother, an old graying Jewess, could have disappeared, like any other Jew, in the camps and possibly would have been melted down for the proverbial German soap factory. He also does this with the conviction that Tom Keeper played his role indirectly, with his evil genius, certainly contributing to the failure of U.S.S. Caine through Maryk who took seriously whatever psychological terms were dished out to him.

Greenwald's sensitive reaction and his concern for humanistic values—he fights for the Indian rights too—force him to take up Maryk's case. Also, being Jewish he knew that if the Nazis were to invade America probably his old mother would be ''melted down'' for the German soap. When he goes to Keeper's party, on the acceptance of his half-finished novel *Multitudes, Multitudes*, he takes him on:

> I defended Steve because I found out the wrong guy was on trial. Only way I could defend was to murder Queeg for you. . . . Queeg deserved better at my hands. I owed him a favour, don't you see? He stopped Hermann Goering from washing his fat behind with my mother.[12]

He throws whisky on Keeper's face and leaves the party. The relevance of this gripping play, a stage version of Herman Wouk's Pulitzer-prize-winning novel of the same name, is that Wouk effectively turns an ordinary court-martial into a Jewish subject, where Greenwald plays a major role. It is not Maryk who is on trial; it is the innocence and ethical loyalties of a person who is taken advantage of by certain clever people like Keeper who may probably write a war novel, in which he can say that the Nazis stink and successfully make money. Greenwald felt that people like him should not be allowed the freedom of his ways. Meanwhile, in Germany, millions of Jews are gassed to death. Greenwald's awareness of the enormity of the evil of the Holocaust and the exploitation of the meek and innocent is the source of his legal victory.

Arthur Miller, it appears, consciously avoids the presentation of the Jews on the stage and when he presents them, their presence is secondary to the general theme of the play. His plays, where the World War is used as background, make use of the theme of Jewish persecution but conclude with some general questions like art and its relation to human ethics and, together, their relation to politics. It even appears that in order to present themes and drive home the central dilemma the War has caused, he makes use of the Jewish experience. Otherwise, he does not discuss Jewish experience on its own terms. By the same token, one can say that since Miller's themes and conclusions are essentially based on Jewish experience, it can still be called a Jewish point of view, for, one cannot exist without the other. However, this is easily an advantage of logical convenience.

For instance, *After the Fall* (1964) introduces "the blasted stone tower of German concentration camp." (12) Its presence in the play can only be called metaphorical and it takes on different meanings: personal, political, mythical and even spiritual. Since the action, as Miller points out, takes place in the mind of Quentin, these aspects have certain relationship with Quentin himself. Here again, Miller, in this autobiographical play, does not discuss the Holocaust as such, nor is the metaphor of concentration camps used effectively. Sometimes it is confusing to the audience as to the presence of the tower itself. In fact, the play can be called a confessional exercise: a patient confessing to the analyst. In this case, the listener acts as a doctor who patiently listens to Quentin's story. But it only ends with his version and the listener—or is it audience?—never has a possibility to respond.

Miller seems to explain McCarthyism, the Communism of the post-war period, and personal guilt associated with his relationships with Maggie, Louise and Felice in terms of the metaphorical use of the concentration camp. Whether his equations are justifiable at all is a matter of argument. Holga always appears with flowers in her hand near the tower. She is not even Jewish, though a communist. Quentine meets her persumably in Germany. No reasons are given as to why he had gone to Germany. Miller's tendency to generalize the Jewish persecution and his conscious avoidance to taking Jewish themes as such is explicit here too. One even wonders that, if only he had made Holga Jewish and a communist, the theme would have been more plausible for it would explain the tragedy that overcame both of them in different ways: the failed attempt of the Communists to overthrow Nazism and the helpless Jews marching into the gas chambers. However when the necessary personal exorcism is over, it is Holga whom he meets suggesting symbolically the union of more than two people which probably suggests the political ideas as well. In fact, the play can also be interpreted as the agony of a liberal who sees everything he believed in crumbling down. Hence, the union of Holga and Quentin can be an acceptance of bruised idealists who have a past of failures and still, having a faith in the future, come together.

Also, by equating the McCarthy era with the massacre of the camps, Miller re-emphasizes the totalitarian mind behind the witch-hunt which forced many people like Lou to commit suicide in order to be faithful to what they stood for, believing in the good of humanity. To buy security for oneself, one has to name names which eventually hurt many people during the plague years. The tower lights up ominously when Lou commits suicide. On the personal side, Maggie has a remote association with the tower, as

Quentin believes, since she cooperated with many men. Quentin even appears to be a symbolic saviour-figure and Maggie a Lazarus-figure. Closely patterned on the life of Marilyn Monroe, the play also focuses on the psychological dimension of a perennially insecure person who felt the absence of a protective father which made a difference in her life to such an extent that she demanded the same protection from every relationship.

These aspects are linked with the myth of the Fall. Quentin realizes that after the bestiality of mass killings and the transgression of man, which is the cause of his expulsion, there still is a possibility for him to face it, "with some gift of courage one may look into its face when it appears, and with a stroke of love—as to an idiot in the house—forgive it."[13] This knowledge of guilt is tellingly brought out with many insights into his personal life and his political commitments. The essential responsibility to himself and to the rest of the mankind once again makes him begin a new life. The union with Holga, as is commented earlier, is more than a personal aspect.

Incident at Vichy (1964) continues the argument of the incongruity of art and morals. Once again the subject is not the Jewish deportation but the fundamental crisis a humanist faces at the dissociation of morals from art. It is the France of 1942 and the German officers pick up some suspects for verification. A left-oriented Bayard gives his interpretation on the situation which blames bourgeoisie. There are other marginal Jews like Monceau, Leduc and Leban and an orthodox old Jew who is unmoved by the reality. As the play progresses, we recognize that it is about Von Berg, an Austrian prince, whose brother, Baron Kessler happens to be a Nazi. A refined man of culture, he is puzzled at the "ocean of vulgarity" implicit in the contemporary moral crisis. Von Berg wonders: "Can people with respect for art go about hounding Jews? Making a prison of Europe, pushing themselves forward as a race of policemen and brutes? Is this possible for artistic people?"[14] It is *the* incident at Vichy. If the play has any significant theme, it is merely this. Von Berg becomes the central figure and his crisis, not the deportation of the Jews as such, is the playwright's concern.

And hence the reason, in terms of dramaturgy, to throw light on Von Berg's problem. Having identified the seminal problem, Von Berg does not know how to find an answer since the reality of the Jewish deportation appears as an anti-thesis, debunking the myth of superior German culture symbolized in German classical western music, philosophy and literature. Von Berg seems to wonder whether these glorified aspects of culture have any relevance unless they bring a sense of dignity and concern to humanity. He also realizes that the credibility of German culture could be questioned unless they emphasize certain ethical standards. In dire need of an explanation, he comes up with the view that the Germans do these atrocious things because they are 'nothing': "They do these things not because they are German but because they are nothing. It is hallmark of the age—the less you exist the more important it is to make a clear impression."[15] For a man who has a moralistic view of art, self-sacrifice is the only source of affirmation so that he can prove to Leduc, who demands responsibility and not merely guilt, and the entire humanity that culture without morals is a contradiction in terms. His sacrifice startles the German Major who seems to recognize the moral of his sacrifice.

Miller's screen play *Playing for Time* (1980), based on a book by Fania Fenelope is an extension of the theme, though it also touches the Jewish problem more meaningfully than the other two plays. One sees the suggestiveness of freight cars, camps and the Nazi bestiality. An effective use of the filmic super-imposition of Dr. Mengele and Fania shows the contrast of art and inhumanity. Fania, taken to the camp from Paris, is forced to sing in the concert for the entertainment of Dr. Mengele. Alma, the leader, knows the price of survival and convinces Fania and others that they have to put up the best performance in order to survive. Esther, a Zionist, questions this compromise of selling their Jewishness for the sake of survival. Although the play's major theme is art and morals, it is significant in that it also appears genuinely concerned about the Jewish problem. The generalized theme does not take away the element of the Jewish angle in the play, possibly because Miller is dramatizing Fania Fenelope's book and, therefore, he cannot take liberties with the text.

It is difficult to explain the generalized approach to a seminal Jewish problem. He had to face severe criticism from engaging critics like Leslie Fiedler and Morris Friedman, the latter convincingly demonstrating the Jewishness in his plays. Whatever may be the reasons for it, one thing is certain: the critics will continue to debate over Miller's lapse in responding to the Jewish issues with a Jewish point of view, instead of projecting his Jewish sense of social justice, guilt and responsibility and, finally, art devoid of moral vision indirectly through non-Jewish characters.

However, there are some plays which take on the challenge of depicting Jewish life during and after the War and some plays even attempt to unravel the dark psyche behind "the final solution." *The Diary of Anne Frank* is one such play. Originally published as *The Secret Annexe* (1947) in the Netherlands, the book is, in fact, a diary published by her father. Later, it was published in America as *Anne Frank: The Diary of a Young Girl* (1952). The playwrights, Frances Goodrich and Albert Hackett, knew that dramatizing a diary certainly creates some problems in terms of dramaturgy. And yet, the audience should be given the impression that it is the diary. This poses the problem of studying the characters mentioned in the diary and present them as such without making them mere characters with no recognizable humanness in them. The playwrights solved this problem brilliantly by introducing a technique which suited their purpose. As each scene comes to an end, the lights dim and Anne's voice is heard as if she is reading aloud her diary. This happens in almost all the scenes. And in the penultimate scene, Anne's voice is cut short in the middle suggesting the deportation of the Franks and the other inmates of the hide-out. The effect is spell-binding which is abundantly shown in the numerous reviews of the play in various countries. In structure, the play is in two acts—each act consists of many scenes.

When the play begins, it is November 1945 and the War is over. Otto Frank, liberated by Allied forces from the camps, comes to Amsterdam. Realizing that his family perished in the camps, he comes to visit the hide-out assisted by Miep. Among many papers,

Miep gets him the diary which he begins to read. Initially, along with Frank's voice, we hear Anne's voice too. And slowly the lights dim. Now, only Anne's voice is heard, as if she were reading her own diary. From here to the penultimate scene of act two, the experience in the hide-out is enacted as a flashback. In a series of scenes, the long journey of the Franks to escape the Nazis is told. At the same time, the process of growing up and the myriad aspects of adolescence are communicated through Anne's understanding of the events. The Franks are joined by Mr. and Mrs. Van Dan and their son, Peter, and later Dussel. During the day, they cannot move about to avoid the suspicion of the employees who work on the ground floor. In the nights, they have to do whatever they can. In the meantime, the gentile friends of the Franks provide rations, information and other necessities.

The play focusses on the personality of Anne who dies before the age of sixteen, and also the evil of the Nazis who massacred the spirit of humanity. Anne emerges as a child of extreme sensitivity, alive to every nuance of life and appears to be popular at her school. Soon she realizes what it means to be in a hide-out. Frank gives her the diary and a piece of advice: "But always remember this, Anneke. There are no walls, there are no bolts, no locks that any one can put on your mind."[16] A sense of uncertainty and the silence of night frightens her. Asked as to what happens if they are found out, Frank tells her that they have to meet with the same fate as the others did. She screams in the night and has nightmares about the Nazis coming to them. Among other things, the play is an enigmatic testimony of what a totalitarian frenzy could do in the name of an approved ideology; more significantly, the impact of such a horror on a growing and sensitive mind. Anne is aware of what others say about her. Other inmates tell her that she is not like Margot. She avoids her mother's presence while glorifying her father, though it hurts her mother. Anne is not unmindful of her behaviour. She even analyzes her behaviour when she confesses to her father that there is always a good Anne and a bad Anne in her but the bad one invariably surfaces to the top while the good one is pushed behind. Anne's love for Peter, the desperate loyalties of one another and the natural instinct for survival at the expense of everything appear to be intermixed with the major themes of Nazi terror and the psychological damage it has done to the child's mind, notwithstanding the education of adolescence. There is no attempt to sentimentalize or exaggerate any experience. There are good gentiles like Miep and Kraloer just as there are people like the doctor who take advantage of their vulnerability and demand more money. Also, even the inmates are presented as the people of flesh and blood with their own weaknesses and selfishness. Mr. Van Dan steals bread and his wife tries to charm Frank. Peter, while being ashamed of his father's behaviour, sticks to him, and decides that if his father is asked to go from the hide-out, he also would go with him.

The other significant factor is the celebration of the Hanukka festival—the festival of lights commemorating the heroic spirit of the Maccabees. It engages the entire scene with the chanting of prayers and the affirmation of their faith in God. This scene, with which the first act ends, stands out as an important aspect of their Jewishness at a time when being Jewish meant massacre and humiliation. As the play goes on, things begin to happen. Peter loses his cat and obviously there is a thief who presumably informs the Nazis about their hiding place for a miserly reward. The gentile friends do not show up. The possibility is that they have been rounded up by the S.S. The Nazis come and take them away. With this flashback completed, the last scene once again is the post-war life—Frank in the hide-out reading the diary. He is reminded by Anne's words that in spite of everything, "I still believe that people are really good at heart."[17] The play concludes with Frank's feeling a sense of shame, possibly because Anne who has perished with the rest of the inmates has faith in humanity while he, having seen so much and suffered so much, has lost faith in it. The play also touches upon the anguish of the survivors. The survivor has to look for other people of his family remotely hoping to meet them. The psychological dimension of such a quiet for all its struggle, would only end in the knowledge of personal loss and tragedy. This is aptly summed up in Frank's experience.

The play has received favourable reviews and won all the

major awards in America including the Pulitzer prize for drama. The lasting significance probably lies in the fact that it has raised serious moral questions pertaining to the Holocaust. This does not ignore the theatrical brilliance and the master craftsmanship of the playwrights who took pains to capture many aspects that a play of this kind must inevitably suggest. Brooks Atkinson writes: ''None of the documents or statistics related to the abominations of the Nazis is so accusing as this diary. It reminds us that the Nazis murdered not only lives but life. They murdered a radiant part of the future.''[11] This is undoubtedly a deserving tribute to the play. It was opened in the seven German cities in November 1956 and broke through the silence with which the Germans treated the Nazi era. In the Netherlands, as a critic of the *New York Times* reports, the audience cried. When the play was over, for some minutes the audience sat in silence. And there was no applause. These incidents prove the impact of the play on the post-war audience and this is suitably supplemented by the international critical response.

The plays that have been discussed so far attempt to face the moral and ethical questions raised by the Holocaust although certain plays like *The Diary of Anne Frank* merely present the child's attitude towards the crisis created by the Nazis. But even here the horror of the times basically takes on a significant perspective for the reason that hitherto cherished values seem to be ineffective to stand firmly against the Nazi extravagances. The plays that are discussed in the following one can convincingly conclude that they do, for the context of the whole situation of the drama, essentially act as a symbolic force on many levels of interpretation. However, these plays concentrated on dramatizing the experience of the camps and how the inmates reacted to the animal kingdom forced on them. None of these plays accepts the conventional dramatic mode of realistic drama. It appears to be their intention that since the Holocaust negated every possibility of definition and ratiocination, the established dramatic technique needs to be replaced by new modes of expression. The techniques they adopted are largely non-realistic with an adept use of recent *avant garde* experiments.

Shimono Wincelberg's *Resort 76* (1981) has made its contribution to these experiments in the theatre. Originally published as *The Windows of Heaven* (1962), the play is based on Rachmil Bryk's novella *A Cat in the Ghetto.* The time of play spans from one Sunday afternoon to Monday morning. The locale is the city of the Lodz in central Poland. *Resort 76* or the rehabilitation zone is part of a grotesque euphemism for a territory which the Nazis occupied and took inhuman measures to put under their control. The focus of the play is on a cat which presumably can provide food and a small job at a ration shop. This allowance is given because the rationshop is infested with rats and mice, and cats could kill them. For the hungry inmates, searching for a cat becomes an obsession and, having found one, they adopt desperate measures to have a share of the cat.

The opening scene—in fact, the background continues to be the same throughout the play—truly reflects the chaos of the times. The suggestiveness of an industrial city, drooping electric wires, factory chimney, the discordant sounds of a harmonica overlapping with other sounds, occasional heavy chugs of the passing rail engines, the old Prussian song and the brickwall scarred by the bullets and shell fragments sum up the waste land. One also realizes the transformation of the symbols of industrial culture. In the process of the play, the contrast between the former symbols of industrial progress like rail engines and factory chimneys become the centres of bestial measures. Also, the intermittent church bells and the whistles of trains complete the dark aural backdrop. The playwright seems to suggest, and the audience undoubtedly can ponder on it, what the church-goers would possibly be praying for or, to put it more meaningfully, what kind of religion could ignore the human degradation that seems to be taking place next door, while the tenets of Christianity are being professed.

Yablonka is a mountebank with red hair, hooded eyes and jaws of a Punch puppet. He stuffs newspapers and straw into his clothing to keep out the cold and walks like a man "kicking dirt into his grave." Blaustain, an engineer, is with a sick pregnant wife. Hauptman is an American businessman and keeps talking about making a successful movie with a human context in war times. This may probably be a satiric comment on many Hollywood movies that supposedly concern themselves with the war themes, though in reality they seem to concoct themes with the backdrop of the second world war which, understandably, fetches enormous benefits. Krause, who is a new entry into their company, is deported to stay with them because he seems to have a Jewish grandfather from his mother's side. His wife threatenes to divorce him unless he makes a confession to the officials, the consequence of which being the present plight. The religious tutor Shnur's presence is not only symbolic but also impressive. He teaches Beryl, the child-pupil, the rules of *shehita*, which, in fact, bothers Blaustain since this concerns itself with the ritual-slaughter of Kosher animals and birds. It also foretells the slaughter of the Jews in the camp and gas chambers. But here there is no religious sanctity nor is there any humane dimension. In fact, the child even asks if human beings can be slaughtered, which is a comment, on the present slaughter. In their conventions, there appears to be a contrast, between the ritual slaughter of Kosher animal and birds and the slaughter of human beings. Even the ritual slaughter demands that the killing should give as little pain as possible whereas the Jews in the camps are forced to experience physical humiliation before they are gassed to death. The heads are shorn, the gold teeth are pulled out and even the clothes are taken and only then they are pushed into the electric ovens. Asked as to why Shnur should teach shehita to a child instead of some useful things like forgery, smuggling and thieving, he replies that he has only the book of ritual-slaughter with him. Krause, on his part, is shocked to see these things which make him comment that this is a world that he has never seen. These inmates work on "textile waste" which is, in fact, torn and bloodstained clothes of the gassed people. They make carpets out of them. Eventually, Krause realizes that tons of gold teeth and trunk-loads of human hair are taken to some other place. Down below their resort, children play with a corpse. Even the plants look different, signifying the deformation of nature. Yablonka knows that as long as they produce effectively, they are allowed to survive. Otherwise, they close down the resort and put them on a train to the gas chambers. Krause reacts to these events rather sensitively and wonders if he has come to a different world altogether. When he starts eating a sandwich Yablonka steps in to polish his shoes and others stare at him for his luxury. However, he comes up with the usual anti-Semitic comment that the Jews killed the Saviour and yet expect them to share their comforts with the Jews. His attitude towards humanity at large and the Jews in particular changes after a series of events especially the incident wherein Beryl's fingers are chopped when he is found digging for sacred books Schnur had buried elsewhere. The boy tells everything under torture. Schnur realizes that there is no escape now. Before he leaves, he convinces Blaustain that he should not kill the child since the breath of a child reading the Law, as the tradition says, brings the Messiah like a whirlwind. He takes off his shoes and gives them to Beryl. Though diffident after the Nazi torture, Beryl regains faith in religion. Later Schnur is taken away. Krause hears the sounds of Schnur being kicked off-stage. In the meantime, he gets a clearance letter which says that his mother was an illegitimate child and that that fact presumably would save him. The play suggests the extreme condition in which these Jews behave and the sacrificing tendency of Schnur and various other demanding situations the other inmates are caught up in. Later Krause goes in and commits suicide. Similarly, there are certain situations that become an acid test to the ethical and moral commitments of human beings. Both Blaustain and Mme. Hersh Kovitch face such situations, though the presence of the cat is the ultimate test of one's own ethical perspective. Blaustain's sister, Anya, asks him to give the cat so that she can arrange assistance to get away from the camps. She appears to be practical in her approach. She even asks him to leave his wife in order to save his life otherwise, she tells him, all of them will perish like their parents. Blaustain withstands these compulsions and sticks to his ethical self while Mme. Hersh Kovitch, stressed by the humanitarian concern to help Blaustain's wife, hesitates at the last moment since she realizes the risks involved in such an act.

Eventually they realize that the cat is of no use. The playwright significantly weaves the dramatic situation around the significance of a cat to suggest the response of people under extreme pressure where life and death depend on their manipulation of possibly the only opportunity. This is also a commentary on the Nazi system which created a social machinery and oppressive means to establish a camp where the human beings are not only treated as animals but are found in situations that can deprive them of their authentic selves. Thus, the words of Yablonka at the end of the play, take on a meaningful tone. He sets the cat free, since the cat has no utility for them, with the following words: ''Go . . . go in peace. . . . Enjoy the sunshine . . . and tell the other animals . . . tell them . . . tell them what it was like to be a Jew.''[19]

Throne of Straw written by Harold and Edith Lieberman continues to depict the realities of the situations and the moral choices of men at a particular moment of time and in particular circumstances. Though so many works have been written about it, the treatment of the story of the Lodze-ghetto through the medium of theatre suggests that the playwrights consciously attempted to find suitable techniques and the means to bring out the enormity of the human factor. And it also works as an example of yet another attempt to capture the perversion of the time in the structure of creative art. The playwrights admit that it is an epic and a folklore: epic in the sense that the events are told in a series of scenes which is characteristic of Greek epics and is folkloric in the Jewish tradition. It is a ''poor'' play and though it admittedly tries to be true to the events, it is not a work of history. And the playwrights confess in a note that their effort is not to judge but to reveal so that each person forms his or her own judgements. Yankele is the play's witness as well as the narrator. His intermittent poems set to music, while serving as useful commentary on the actual events, would also function as a Brechtian technique of alienation. Otherwise the central focus is on Rumkowski, the eldest of the Lodz Jewish Council, and his attempts to save the Jewish community. An ardent Zionist and popularly known as the Father of Orphans in the pre-war era, he thinks that he is responsible only to God for his actions.

Rumkowski convinces Biebow that they should run factories

and the orphanage to help the starving masses, though in achieving it he had to do some humiliating acts. Consequently, he succeeds in preserving a degree of order only to yield to the pressures of the Nazis eventually. The deportations increase continuously. He saves the Wolf family from extinction for a moment for the sake of Ada who seems to fascinate him. He believes that it is difficult to fight against the mighty forces and that, with argument and bargaining, at least a small number of the Jews can be saved. He also knows about the fate of the other ghettoes which disappeared because of their attempts at resurgence. Israel Wolf, an old Jew, keeps the record of his reaction to the events, throwing light on the dubious ways of both Nazis and Rumkowski.

Together with Yankele's comments, Wolf's diary provides a decisive insight into the painful days beset by moments of moral choices and physical survival. Ada, his daughter, knows quickly that to survive she has to charm not only Rumkowski but, once his power is on the decline, also the next person who takes his place in power. Rosa, her daughter, does not appreciate the special favour done to their family and, being a Communist, does not believe in cooperating with the Germans in the false hope of survival. She feels that they should wage war against them through affordable means like going on strike and non-cooperation. As it turns out, neither Rumkowski nor the Communists like Rosa could save the Jews. Each of them believed in his or her strategies in the face of physical extinction. Within no time Rumkowski loses credibility from the Nazis's point of view and, moved by the fact that one of his orphan boys is being deported, he also chooses to join others. The Wolf family which has been effectively protected by Ada, also joins the deportees. As Yankele says in the conclusion of the play there are two sides of Rumkowski's last days. Some say that he finally took his place at the end of the line to the gas chambers, and others believe that he is thrown in first. What is significant in the play is the playwrights's persistent attempt to explore the techniques in order to dramatize the usable past and available history.

To this end, Yankele's poems and his commentaries are useful. This play begins with his prologue on the "passion play" of the Jewish persecution. The locale is Oberammergau, the home of the Christian passion play. It is a town in Bavaria where the passion play is staged every ten years. The text, till recently, was believed to be fundamentally anti-Semitic. The spotlight picks Yankele in a crucifixion posture. And he speaks to the audience, not about the passion of Jesus Christ but the predicament of the Jews in Diaspora. He has a series of poems addressed to the audience which, while commenting on many historical events, focus on the personalities of Rumkowski and others. In fact, the title of the play is a metaphor used to suggest the paradoxical implications of Rumkowski's position, while Yankele's poems comment on, among other things, important historical subjects like court Jew or council Jew. The very idea of the court Jew is to use certain Jews to control the rest of the Jews in a particular ghetto. This serves two purposes: one, the blame for atrocious actions falls on the court Jew and second, the overlord can conveniently get his things done whether it is collecting large amounts of money or making them victims of anti-Semitism for any calamity that befalls the state. Also, Yankele's episode of Maimonides touches the painful moral tension that beset the Jewish experience over the centuries. When the elders of the Jewish community go to him for his advice on the necessity that an innocent be turned over to the enemies so that at least the remnant of this community can survive, Maimonides says that the rest of them should join him. But their comments will raise the central issues related to the archetypal Jewish predicament:

> Rabbi Maimonides, if we do as you suggest
> How will a remnant be saved?
> But on the other hand
> If we don't do as you say
> What kind of remnant will it be?[20]

These words echo the moral and ethical aspects advocated by rabbinic Judaism on the one hand and, on the other, the messianic dream promised by the divine presence. It also touches, if indirectly, the implicit urge to survive and hopes to realize the dream of messianic aspirations.

These are the major aspects of the play. It comes to a close with Yankele talking to the audience. His final comments are an admonition to the audience. Talking about the "passion play"—passion of the Jewish community in the Diaspora—he warns them not to feed him with "dinner talk morals" as to what they should have done. Instead, he advises them to ask themselves what they could have done in similar circumstances. These words said, he asks the audience that since the shrouds of the dead have no pockets and the ashes have no permanent home, where one should keep them. These words have a Zionist implication when he stresses the "permanent home." His final comments warn not to indulge in easy morals. This needs to be explained for there are some books in the post-war era which did attempt at such an indulgence. Whatever may be the merits of Hannah Arendt's *Eichman in Jerusalem*, she certainly spoke about how the Jews meekly accepted the victim roles. She does not make any complimentary remarks on Judenraat for the reason that these Jewish councils facilitated the journey to the gas chambers.

George Tabori's *The Cannibals* is yet another example of the artistic problems that the Holocaust poses. Like the two Lodze plays, *The Cannibals* is also predominantly a poignant instance of technical innovation. It shares the influence of the Brechtian theory of alienation with *Throne of Straw*. It is primarily a story of the dinner party in the camps, told by the sons of the participants who perished in the camps except Heltai and Hershler who, much against the will of the Uncle, eat the soup made of human flesh, for the sake of survival. When the play opens, the war is over and the relatives and sons of the deceased come to pick the clothing of the deceased. They come with grey make-up. The voices in the loudspeakers call for their favourite dishes. For a moment, they look like the inmates. They blow the ram's horn and freeze. Heltai and Hershler, the survivors, talk about their present lives. Heltai still likes banana split and Hershler has set up practice. Then he bows to the audience and tells them about themselves. Out of the twelve inmates they alone could survive. The next scene takes us to the camp life. Thus, the flashback brings out their struggle for life in a series of scenes which underline the essential absurdity and the grotesque reality which is thrust upon them. But then, the story is the enactment of the facts provided by the two survivors to the sons of the dead inmates. Each of the sons, having performed the roles of their fathers, profusely bows to the audience with a few comments from him. They not only play the roles but also provide their own comments on the situation. So the story of Puffi's death and cooking of his body for the inmates's dinner is brilliantly told with grim humour. Pantomime is used and the banal themes like sodomy, and scatological comments are made part of the story manipulated to tell the grotesque reality which is part of such a circumstance.

Uncle is a religious man who denounces the meal of human flesh. Being a professional actor, he takes a vow not to speak at all. When he starts praying to God, others form a God-figure. And Klaub plays the role of God. Each of the inmates plays different roles in varying contexts of episodes and situations. And there will be a series of enactments of various incidents. Thus, the Gypsy enacts the murder he has committed, others perform various types of deaths. Uncle seems to apply the analogy of the Hebrews complaining to Moses after their liberation from Egypt to that of the inmates committing abomination by eating human flesh. Even religion does not escape its role in the pattern of their black humour. He makes comments on the theme of non-resistance, pacifism and tolerance to the extent of showing the other cheek. The end of the Age of Reason also is noted with sarcasm for they seem to suggest that the death camps and the monstrous mind which justified it is an extension of the Enlightenment in the sense that an excessive emphasis on rationalism and the centrality of man in the scheme of things forces an added advantage to the myth of superman which, in turn, fascinated even the enlightened people. Consequently, the methods of Hitler and his attempt to take advantage of the age-old German myths is tolerated even when it smacked of violence. It is little wonder that Uncle, the central figure of the play, curses the language and tells the Kid, an amateur actor, that he is the "rapist of the word." Further he also comments: "I refused to use something that was being abused, I was on strike against these hysterics, these whores, the thieves who plucked the purest words out of our languages—Glory! Honor! Freedom!—when all they meant was—kill them."[21] This partly explains why these playwrights depend on non-verbal techniques to a large extent, although writing about the situation of the camps and their inmates coupled with their ways of facing the morbid reality also poses problems in the creative process of the language.

In the penultimate scene Uncle is put on trial because he asked his inmates not to eat human flesh, at a time when only this could save them from the "shower" room. They fall upon him and strip him naked. The ram's horn is heard and they step back. Then Uncle desperately tells them that he is not Uncle, but his son playing his role. He reminisces about his father who used to hate flesh and, then, ponders over the idea of God's creation and comes to the conclusion that He has failed miserably or He is not right in feeling happy about his creation. It is time, he feels, he started all over again. The fact that even the sons who play the roles of their fathers, in a frenzy, strip Uncle naked shows that what they did was an inevitable consequence. There are enactments within enactments. The last scene again takes us back to the survivors, this time joined by Schrekinger's son who also enacts a scene between him and his father. He enacts the conversation between him and his father, playing both the roles. The son asks what he has done during the war—a question that has since been haunting the children of the fathers who are associated with the War. Instead of answering his questions, he talks about how he was simply following orders. Further, he says that by meekly doing whatever they were asked to do, the Jews remained pure pointing the finger towards evil though it is "fashionable to say that they did not fight back, did not resist."[22] Exasperated, the son throws a chair at his father. He actually does it in the enactment too. Then, Hershler talks to the audience. He talks about his usual visits to the analyst. The moment he goes to him the doctor turns off his hearing aid and Hershler has to holler his banalities at him. Heltai immediately plays the role of the analyst. Hershler had had dreams of a dead child in a rice paddy and he was happy. The analyst thinks he is unhappy which is the normal response. It makes him happy because this proves to him that everybody is a murderer like him who ate the flesh of man in order to survive. Like the son Schrekinger, Hershler also hits the analyst. After a while, the former climbs on the table and starts wolfing down supposedly human flesh. And this act is followed by the orchestra, and the loudspeakers are heard talking about Herodotus who wrote the tale of "the Sythian Marragetae/who killed old people and ate them."[23] The voice in the loudspeakers advises the "dear brethren in Christ" to eat the Jew's heart so that they also can escape from the ghosts of Jews which is a superstitious practice among primitive savages.

This may be an indictment against Christianity itself. It can also be interpreted that the Christian anti-Semitism points out in the note that the site is "nowhere... the place that no one can imagine" and it is a "desolate landscape . . . in a light of unreality."[24] The position and movements of the characters are suggested only by the lighting. There is no make up except that the faces are powdered grey. And the play is without intermission to sustain the impact of the theme. With all these innovations in technique, it also conforms to a certain extent to the well-made play. It has a prologue and an epilogue spaced in between by three acts. The camp experience is told in flashback, for in the prologue Francoise says that she returned to tell the truth. Each act is loaded with a series of scenes in collage fashion. Sometimes, long declamations are used as in Greek drama. While many of the inmates perished, only Francoise and Denise are alive but they seem to face the problem of language because they "came from a place where words had a different meaning,"[25] and the simple words like cold, thirst, hunger and sleep have a different implication altogether. They are aware that it is unbelievable to others just as it is to themselves. The play ends with question:

> Why should you believe
> those stories of ghosts

> ghosts who came back and who are not able
> to explain how?[26]

While apparently functioning within the schema of the well-made play, it seems to negate the arrogance implicit in this structure, that it can capture every human dimension of life. One wonders why these playwrights are so engrossed in experimenting with multiple techniques to find a suitable communication. There is also a danger of extolling their techniques at the expense of the theme. Primarily they seem to question the myths of order in human existence *per se*. These attempts, on their part, the babbling of the characters and the tyranny of non-communication, however, underline their intended view. If there is a moral at all, it may be simply this: the Holocaust exists as a watermark between the pre-Holocaust civilization and the post-Holocaust era as Raul Hilberg rightly points out in *Destruction of the European Jews* (1961):

> Simply as a fact and as a precedent it mocks our desire to affirm life's goodness and undermines our hope that never again will human beings gather in such vast and well ordered numbers to commit mass murder. It stands as a proof of the human potential for radical evil and therefore also as prophecy of our possible future.[27]

To sum up what has been discussed in this chapter, it is evident that the Jewish playwrights have shown an anti-war stance in their war plays. This may be explained in the traditional Jewish passion for peace which has the ratification of the biblical vision, the Rabbinic Judaism coupled with the experience of the pariah-role the Jews have been playing through the centuries. Their ghetto existence both in Europe and elsewhere is intermittently troubled with violence and killings. The growing anti-Semitism in the thirties and with the emergence of Hitler, who expertly manipulated the rhetoric of anti-Semitism talking about the superiority of the Aryan race, must be a reason for the anti-war theme which is not always different from the theme of anti-Semitism since it is generally associated with the destroyers of peace and liberal values.

However, the Holocaust changed the literary horizon to such an extent that the idea of artistic creation is haunted by moral and ethical questions. At no point of time in the history of creative art have such complex questions been asked. While facing the enormous burden of being truthful to the violence of the Holocaust, the writer and especially the survivor has felt a responsibility to tell the story of human degradation. Though survivors like Elie Wiesel maintained silence for sometime, the need to tell the world what it meant to be there brought them to a viewpoint that necessarily resulted in their insights into the Holocaust. Drama has its share in the contribution to this end. For once, one surmises, the artistic sense of reality and the reality in historical terms seem to coincide and go hand in hand, though the authors certainly exercised selection in order to arrive at certain conclusions. There is also a danger, in this endeavour, to think or to take it for granted that whatever they have communicated through their art could be the only view which may lead to theoretical complications and sometimes even to a heresy of misconceptions. However, the attempts of the playwrights could be meaningful if we keep these views in mind and then look at their presentation of reality.

No doubt these playwrights have meddled with varieties of techniques—starting from the well-made play to the *avant garde*. While certain plays predominantly accepted the conventional mode of the well-made play; a structure to portray the dimension of human agony and the realistic overview of the circumstances that forced them to respond in myriad ways, whenever they had to depict the life in the camps they broke the norms and techniques of structure and liberally introduced techniques from the Greek choric declarations, Brechtian alienation, pantomime, and even black humour. If the survivors have faced the problem of putting into words what they have been in the camps, the creative writers also had the problem of imaginatively perceiving the Holocaust, influenced to a large extent by his knowledge gained from the available literature on this subject. For these writers and also for the survivors, the legacy of the Holocaust is a gigantic negation of form and expression. This resulted in the breaking of the conventional patterns, since the Holocaust has destroyed history as a concept and humanity as a recognizable paradigm evocative of a sense of justice and universal brotherhood. This is possibly the only explanation one can think of for a series of experiments that one can find in the works depicting the life in the camps, though Elie Wiesel himself stuck to conventional narrative in his novella called *Night.* It is difficult to recreate the atmosphere of the camp in realistic patterns and hence the reason for the non-realistic techniques making use of every possible theatrical mode including even music to make up for the inadequacy of the word. These experiments have emerged as an enigmatic testimony to the crimes perpetrated against man in the name of an ideology which had built its rhetoric and rationale from every available source, even quoting from the musical genius, Richard Wanger.

These creative writers are successful in voicing the inhumanity of the Holocaust and the frenzy of anti-Semitism. While reflecting on the view that the Holocaust destroyed what is respectable and dear to humanity, they also questioned the arrogance of man in placing himself above the animal kingdom, though he had proved over and over again that he could be worse than the animals. They seem to raise some fundamental questions and wonder if man is justified at all in weaving theories around man's presence in history and his role in shaping it, and also the view that man is the measure of all things as Renaissance humanism so unmistakably emphasized in the oft-quoted Protagorian dictum. From the Renaissance to the Holocaust, the story of man appears to have come full circle. As always in the history of human civilization the image of the Jew once again became a cataclysmic factor, which raises some of the serious questions that haunt the post-Holocaust era and, the reality of which, becomes the backdrop for the modern literary tradition.

NOTES

1. Franz Kafka, *The Complete Stories*, ed. Nahum Glatzer (New York: Schocken, 1971), p. 4.
2. Isaac Rosenfeld, *An Age of Enormity* (Cleland: World, 1962), p. 33.
3. Elie Wiesel in *Confronting the Holocaust,* ed. Alvin H. Rosenfeld (Bloomington: India University Press, 1978), p. 4.
4. Lawrence Langer, *Versions of Survival* (Albany: The University of New York Press, 1982), p. 1.
5. Rolf Hochhuth, *The Deputy, Best Plays of 1963-64,* ed. Henry Hewes (New York: Dodd Mead and Company, 1964), p. 258.
6. *Ibid.*, p. 266.
7. *Ibid.*, p. 278.
8. Robert Shaw, *The Man in the Glass Booth, The Best Plays of 1968-1969,* ed. Guemsey, Jr. (New York: Dodd, Mead and Company, 1969), pp. 212-13.
9. Ronald Ribman, *Cold Storage, Five Plays* (New York: Avon, 1978), p. 336.
10. *Ibid.*
11. *Ibid*, p. 339.
12. Herman Wouk, *The Cain Mutiny Court-Martial* (New York: Doubleday, 1954), p. 128.
13. Arthur Miller, *After the Fall, Collected Plays*, Vol. II (New York: The Viking Press, 1981), p. 241.
14. Arthur Miller, *Incident at Vichy, Collected Plays,* Vol. II, p. 260.
15. *Ibid.*, pp. 269-70.
16. Frances Goodrich and Albert Hackett, *The Diary of Anne Frank* (New York: Random House, 1956), p. 26.
17. *Ibid.*, p. 174.
18. Brooks Atkinson in the Introduction to *Anne,* p. ix.
19. Shimon Wincelberg, *Resort 76, The Theatre of the Holocaust* (Wisconsin: The University of Wisconsin Press, 1982), p. 112.
20. Harold Edith and Liberman, *Throne of Straw, Theatre of the Holocaust*, p. 148.
21. George Tabori, *The Cannibals, The Theatre of the Holocaust,* p. 231.
22. *Ibid.*, p. 263.
23. *Ibid.*, p. 264.
24. Chrlotte Delbo, *Who Will Carry the Word?*, *Theatre of the Holo-*

caust, p. 269.

25. *Ibid.*, p. 324.
26. *Ibid.*, p. 325.
27. Raul Hilberg, *Destruction of the European Jews* (New York: Quadrangle Books, 1961), p. 760.

Hebraic Humanism: The Bible and Jewish American Drama

> For the Jew, Judaism is the only possible way to humanism. It stresses human relations even more than God-man relations. There is no word, for example, in Hebrew, the sacred tongue, for the atheist. . . . The closest term would be *Kofer be' ikor,* "Someone who denies the essential" or God. But if we check the Talmudic sources we see that whenever the term appears it deals with relation between man and man or man and woman, not with God. Whoever betrays humanity, whoever torments one's fellowman, denies the existence of God.[1]

These words of Elie Wiesel, who is a pre-eminent voice in the post-Holocaust era, not only emphatically point out the humanistic fervor embedded in Judaism but also touches upon its ethical culture and mutual responsibility of human beings. It is also significant that there is no equivalent of the word "atheist" in Hebrew. The approximate description, as Wiesel affirms, is in the context of the relationship between man and man rather than man and God which unquestionably has been the primary concern of Judaism, for, it considers that sin against the fellow-human beings is a sin against God. Once this clarification is accepted, even some of the non-believing humanists like Marx, Spinoza and, in recent years, Marcuse and Erich Fromm could be positively explained within the tradition for their humanism, though they certainly pay little attention to the matters concerning God.

When Elie Wiesel says that for a Jew his religion is the only means of humanism, he is not overstating the influence of the Jewish faith. Instead, he is merely explicating a fact that since the ethical aspects are so dear to Judaism and the concepts of individual and collective moral behaviour and social justice are as old as the Hebrew Bible, the Jew, in fact, has no better introduction to these matters than his religion itself. The Hebrew Bible classified into three categories called the Torah, the Prophets and the Writings, is not the only document. There is the Talmud also which comprises the rabbinic wisdom of centuries and which reflects their responses to the changing times of different cultures and from which the rabbinic dedication to Judaism and their faith in Jews as a People of the Book, preserved their separate identity. Rabbinic Judaism put the Jewish people together when they were forced to live in ghettoes and thus was instrumental in establishing a sense of communal life with a strong manifestation to the biblical spirit. Yiddish literature breathes of Talmudic Judaism. The ghetto is a world in itself imbued with the spirit of the Bible thanks to the Halakah (the law) which has been the guiding force to the rabbis who are the heads of the community. Sholom Aleichem, in his inimitable humour, paints the picture of European *Shtetl* life in his stories. The influence of the Bible is all-pervading in Yiddish literature as is obvious in the works of I.L. Peretz, Mendele Mokher Sforim, Sholom Ash and a host of others that followed them. While some took an ironic and didactic view, others found a satiric vein in the lives of *Yiddishkeit*. Written for the Jews of the *shtetl*, their works rarely stepped beyond the concerns of everyday predicament of Jews owing to the external prejudices. Their confined existence made them conscious of their exclusiveness and they knew that chosenness coupled with religious misunderstanding was the reason for their tribulations. And they went on explicating the biblical contexts with contemporary social situations tempered considerably with Yiddish folklore so that the common folk could understand and wonder at God's riddles. The Enlightenment broke the walls of the ghetto and the Jews began to participate in the mainstream social life which, in due course of time, gave them the opportunity to express their creative vision in different languages. This posed a serious problem, for as long as the creative writing is meant for only the Jews, the thematic concerns with a religious view that occupy Yiddish literature can be appreciated. Further, the life in the ghettoes which was the subject matter of their literature is no longer available. The winds of change and the fact that since they are writing in the language of the gentiles and the possibility that they may be read by non-Jews also, who may not know anything about the Jewish religion, brought up a new set of both thematic and structural problems. How the Jewish writers negotiated the challenge of the situation is a different story. The Jewish writers of America especially are successful in creating a Jewish sensibility in their works though in poetry the early attempts of Charles Reznikoff—whose endeavour has been not only to write about the Jewish themes largely influenced by the Bible but also to create a medium which could suit the themes—are not effectively followed by the succeeding generation of poets. But in fiction, short story and even in poetry, their success deserves recognition. With this overview, it will be worthwhile to analyze the biblical plays, written in Yiddish and English, in order to see the different situational aspects, though, as it so often happens, the essential theme is humanistic, communicated through the biblical episodes.

Chaim Sloves's *Haman's Downfall* is based on a biblical story from the book of Esther. Married to a gentile king, Ahasuerus, she comes to know that Haman wants to destroy the entire Jewish community. Later with the help of Mordecai, her uncle, she creates a situation which not only convinces the king that Haman is a villain but also that the Jews are harmless victims of his political ambitions. Esther is forever glorified for her heroism in Purim—a Jewish festival commemorating the event. The original story is adapted to the oldest Jewish theatre form called *Purim-shpil.*

The play begins with a prologue and is followed by four acts. The Herald greets the audience in the prologue and tells them that the play is "true and comical" and then goes on introducing the characters of the play. Having introduced Ahasuerus, Mordecai, Esther, Haman, he asks all of them to leave the stage so that they can march and dance to the music of the conductor. All of them joyfully dance to the music. Similarly, the Herald reads from the scroll before every act and the theme of what he has read is enacted by the characters. As the play unfolds, the allegorical element asserts itself. The play was written during the Nazi period. Haman who, according to the biblical episode, hatched a conspiracy to kill the Jews and dethrone Ahasuerus is Hitler of the modern times. Symbolically, the predicament of the Jews is mediated by Mordecai and Esther who tactfully educate the king to such an extent that he can see the conspiracy and danger not only to his position but also to his life. Consequently, he punishes Haman and the Jews are rewarded suitably.

The story is dramatized with situations that are essentially Jewish. Mordecai is a *shadchan,* a matchmaker, who initially saves the king from Haman's plot and then plays the role of a matchmaker in arranging a marriage between the king and Esther, though the latter does not seem to be much interested. And the marriage is performed according to the Jewish rituals. The play is filled with many humorous scenes, sometimes bordering on the bawdy. For instance, the scenes between Ahasuerus and Vashti and when the king decides to desert her, are examples of this kind. Mordecai, on his part, is made to look like a drunkard though he has a commitment to his people. Haman also has his due of pranks and takes advantage of the king's foolishness in getting ratification to exterminate the Jews and even making an attempt to blackmail the queen for her Jewish origin.

The propaganda that the Jews are corrupt and have a corrupting influence on their society brings to mind the Nazi propaganda itself which is intended by the playwright. The conclusion spells the message of the play in Mordecai's words. Haman is punished and the Jews are saved which optimistically suggests that the Jewish persecution in Germany could be a temporary phase and the new Haman, that is Hitler, would also face the same end as the biblical Haman did. Mordecai says that "there is no superior race! All are equal! Anyone caught mistreating a Hebrew will follow Haman to his ancestors!"[2] Later, he promises peace to the kingdom unlike Haman who stupidly wages war against the Greeks for no cause beyond imperialistic frenzy of power. Then, the Herald comes and declares that the *Purim-shpil* is over.

For a drama critic, this kind of play certainly poses a problem of classification. Although it is a play of seriousness, the humorous strain continues to entertain—even burlesque humour is introduced. The Herald's introduction reminds one of the Brechtian alienation since the audience knows that they are, after all, characters. And the heroic aspects of certain characters like Mordecai and Esther and the treacherous villainy of Haman is played down since they too participate, to a certain degree, in the situational humour. The characters address the audience also on some occasions. More significantly, the Yiddish folklore form makes the play lively and entertaining. The Jewish humour keeps the oft-repeated tale a refreshingly entertaining one. Finally, though the play is given a Jewish context of the Diaspora, the message is that of the danger of mass psychosis and personal megalomania which could take advantage of the available social literature and the vulnerabilities of the established prejudices to force an extreme ideology irrespective of human disaster even when it hurts the innocent people of a particular religious persuasion. The biblical context is used to comment on the contemporary society. Even the language is modern in every scene and the allegory is well-established.

Arthur Miller's *Creation of the World and Other Business* (1972) is not an allegory. Instead, Miller attempts to present the narration of the creation from *Genesis* of the Bible and thereby not only establish God-man relationship but also mutual responsibility among human beings. The play has a regular Jewish family pattern. The familiar Jewish humour patterned into a family situation with ultimate cosmic profundity is truly within the Jewish tradition. The play has Miller's familiar themes which are extended from the earlier plays. The unworldly father, practical mother, and the visionary and well-meaning grandfather of Yiddish literature are aptly presented in the play. When the play opens, Adam is already created. And the sounds of birds and animals make the scene cacophonous. God arrives and helps Adam to name things. When God mentions that all creatures are in pairs, Adam is quick to say that he is glad that God talked about this. After some humorous talk in a matter-of-fact tone God tells him that sometimes things happen without much thinking on His part. For instance Adam is created out of the remaining clay after the creation of the chimpanzee. Later, God convinces Adam that He would create Eve and assures him that "You don't have to hang around her every minute. If it gets too much, you just walk off by yourself."[3] After the creation of Eve, God tells them that they should not eat the apple from the Tree of Knowledge. Eve asks for the reason immediately, symbolic of her rational self which is expertly taken advantage of by Lucifer. Lucifer's role in the play is impressive in the sense that he, with his evil-minded logic, brings a lively atmosphere in terms of drama for it is because of his moves and manoeuvres in dethroning God and taking revenge against God by destroying His beloved creation that the cosmic drama takes a lively shape though the play as such leaves many matters unclarified regarding certain thematic concerns. Lucifer even tries to convince God that He should give the same kind of holy feeling to sex as Adam has towards Him. And absence of curiosity towards the Tree of Knowledge, Lucifer says, is the reason for his inability to think in terms of multiplying. For Lucifer's arguments in favour of, what later became, Adam's fall, God gives the reasons for planting the tree and prohibiting Adam and Eve from eating its fruit. When God created man, He felt so overjoyed that He liked Adam more than anything He had ever created and, for a moment, felt the tempting idea that "may be I should let him see through the rose petal to its chemistry. . . . His simple praise for surfaces made me impatient to share with him the physics of My art which would raise him to a God."[4] But He recollects what became of Lucifer who cannot take a "breath without thinking how to overthrow Me and take over the Universe!"[5] With these words that the knowledge makes them forget God, He walks off only to leave Lucifer thinking that since he is the corrective factor, he wants to fulfil God's inner urges. And then follows the fall of man and banishment. The moment they eat the forbidden fruit, Eve asks God as to why he has put the tree there when He does not expect them to eat the fruit. Adam says that he is ignorant and does not deserve the punishment. However, God is overjoyed at the news that they are multiplying which, once again, paves the way for yet another dialogue between God and Lucifer where Lucifer proposes, after a clever argument, that they should share the world—with Lucifer as the Minister of Excremental Matters for they are "the two inseparable buddies."[6] God, for the last time, makes a distinction that where evil begins He ends. God refuses Lucifer's perversion, and Lucifer leaves to destroy God's creation further.

Although Lucifer is fairly successful in his attempts to introduce Eve to sin, God returns them to innocence once again after the birth of Cain. God even dances with Eve which pleases Adam. While all of them dance with joy, Lucifer kisses Cain and once again Lucifer is determined to use Cain for his evil purposes.

When the last act begins, Adam already has two sons. God feels that once again the human beings are on the verge of forgetting Him forever. So, He asks Azrael to send the dreams of death so that they can remind them of the inevitable end and bring them back to God's ways. Adam and Eve discuss the bad dream with Cain and Abel. Cain feels that his parents must have committed a transgression and hence this is a sign of a curse. Thus begins the first sabbath in order to praise God. Cain, the originator of the Sabbath, also asks Adam why they could not have multiplied in the Garden, a pertinent question that reminds one of God's comments when Lucifer implies that the eating of the fruit is necessary to multiply. Soon they prepare offerings to God. And God prefers Abel's lamp while merely accepting Cain's onion for which he tirelessly laboured. Lucifer senses murder in the family which, he reasons, brings in Father Guilt that may haunt mankind forever and which is necessary to bring man to think of God and the significance of His presence. In the absence of God, man can do anything. Despite Lucifer's attempts Cain kills Abel. Cain asks God to save them from this curse. As God explains, it is a chance for Cain to walk in God's ways and forget the jealousy he has towards Abel: "I saw that Cain was pious, yet in him I saw envy too. And so I thought—If Cain was so enraged that he lift his hand against his brother, but then, remembering his love for Abel and for me, even in his fury lay down his arms? You would have risen like a planet before the generations . . . first brother and the first to reject murder.''[7] Vexed with the business of man's creation, God asks Lucifer to take over the realm of mankind but Lucifer, for all his criticism, cannot create. Mercifully, Adam realizes, as he always does, that Lucifer cannot have them. And God puts a mark on Cain's face which can save him from danger and tells them that from now on they have to look for God in themselves and he would never return. Eve is unhappy about Abel's death, the reasons for which she can never understand. Cain refuses to ask her pardon in spite of Adam's insistence. Desperately Adam asks Eve to cry mercy in God's name for the human situation is so precarious. Adam's final words are significant: ''Cain, we are surrounded by beasts! And God's not coming any more. . . . Boy, we are all that's left responsible!'' (106) A greater responsibility on the first family of mankind, but Cain does not yield to his request. And the play ends with ''roars, songs, and cries of the animals.'' (106) And Adam and Eve walk on to the periphery, Adam with his arm around Eve, and Eve struggling to speak but not able to and instead, weeping. Adam in Eve's name cries mercy. Cain, unmoved, leaves without remorse.

The play troubles many in terms of Miller's intention in retelling the biblical episode. One could even say that Miller merely wrote the play in the true Yiddish tradition with Jewish humour in the quintessential Jewish family setting. Miller has angered many critics for the ethnic anonymity of his plays though many critics have clearly established the Jewishness of his plays. Daniel Walden, in a different context, and certainly in view of this play, writes: ''It seems undesirable that in attempting to deal with his moral dilemma, Miller's roots were the barb or spur reflecting his Jewish heritage and sensitivity, and responsible for his continuity of thought and treatment from Brooklyn to Broadway, from adolescence to *Death of a Salesman.*''[8] It could be argued that the same thematic concerns are implicit in the present play too, although the dramatic intensity of the moral dilemma and the degree of Jewish heritage can be debatable. It is the moral question for Eve till the close of the play, for she cannot find a reason as to why an innocent and God-fearing person has to be killed. God's interpretation that in order to test Cain's love for God and hence for God's creation may work as a restricting force in Cain's jealous act, does not convince Eve at all, for, once again, she seems to rationalize that, after all, Abel has become a victim of God's testing practices and Abel is an innocent man. And probably this is the reason why she does not cry mercy when Adam insists that she should. She is not sure of God's designs, not to think about God's implementation of His divine will.

The play leaves many aspects unclarified. Sometimes it gives the impression that God is uncertain and vacillating about the business of creation. When God creates the first human beings, Lucifer comes up with the villainous argument that if God does not want Adam and Eve to eat the apple, why he should plant the tree there at all. Despite God's warnings Lucifer does the damage for which act Lucifer is thrown out of heaven. And almost immediately God seems to feel for the absence of Lucifer. To give another example, Adam is happy when God mentions that all beings live in pairs in paradise though, asked by God if it disturbs Adam that he is alone, Adam does not explain properly what he feels. Only the conclusion of the play touches Miller's humanism especially when Adam talks about the mutual responsibility at a time when almost everything is menacing. In the last analysis, this may be Miller's message in the play. Otherwise, it is a regular Jewish family story told in the strain of situational comedy. Jewish humour keeps the play alive to a certain extent. The only theological aspect seems to be that while Lucifer's designs are pointed at ultimate subversion, Miller implies that there is still a possibility of something good that can emerge from the intended evil acts, which results in grace and a sort of return to Eden at least in spirit that Adam and Eve acquire after their "fall." The fall is engineered by Lucifer and yet they regain innocence at the end of the play. Also, the concepts of sin and the Fall have been dramatized according to the Jewish tradition. In this connection, Robert Gordis's views expressed in *Judaism for the Modern Age* aptly embody Miller's views:

> Judaism never maintained the view that man's nature is innately evil. Nor did it seek to buttress the doctrine that Adam's sin of disobedience in the Garden of Eden placed a hereditary and unavoidable taint upon all his descendants. . . . On the contrary, the basic Hebrew standpoint is expressed in the admonition to Cain that sin always is in wait for man, but that he can rule over it.[9]

Coming to the response to the play, critics did not approve of the dramatization. While appreciating type talent of actors and setting, many of them felt that the play did not come through impressively. Richard Watts in *New York Post* says that the play "appeared to me uncertain of the viewpoint it was driving at and far from clear about its aim."[10] Stanley Kauffmann's comments are pertinent: "Miller does not know what he wants to say. He improvises and patches, in speech that mixes borscht and the Bible. This suggests one more evasion with which Miller might be indicted, his evasion of Jewishness in his career. Many have noted that tonalities of speech and character in *The Death of a Salesman* are Jewish, yet Miller refused to acknowledge this. There are clues all through the play that it was meant to be a Jewish domestic comedy on Biblical themes."[11]

In retrospect, it appears that critics have been a little too severe on Miller. Whatever may be the vagueness, one thing could be said in favour of the author. While following the tradition of Jewish comedy with a biblical setting, he reflects the Jewish situational humour; and his views on certain key concepts faithfully reflect the Jewish viewpoint. If one has to find a predominant humanistic voice, it is man's wonderment and painful awareness, his dilemma at God's riddles, as one sees in Eve and Cain and the undeniable moral standpoint, that human beings should stick together in the time of crisis. Miller's humanism is expressed through the biblical play although the conclusion can be interpreted either in terms of pessimism since Cain does not accept Adam and the screaming animal voices symbolically suggest something evil, or in accordance with the need for a greater commitment since the times are treacherous for man.

Based on the biblical Flood, Clifford Odets's *The Flowering Peach* (1954) does not have any thematic inconsistency. Odets puts much of his personality coupled with his agonies after his appearance before the House of Un-American Activities committee during the days of McCarthyism. This play is a regular Jewish family story, perhaps more Jewish than Miller's, since the Jewish rituals like Shabbos and explicit behaviour of Noah similar to that of an Old Country Jew with Yiddish-English inflexions are, once again, a common feature as in Odets's other plays.

The play is about "then, not now," which is enough of a suggestion that the personal history of the author is understandable. The episode of Noah's family is told in a series of scenes, beginning at Noah's house where he has a dream about the Flood and human disaster and, later, the life on the Ark and the conclusion when the Ark reaches the shore. In between the good-natured bantering of Noah and Esther and Japheth's untiring question to God for the destruction of mankind and the situational aspects of Shem and Ham—these matters become the subject which has been woven into a typical Jewish story.

Noah, like Adam in the *Creation,* is a *Schlemiel*-figure. When he has the dream it worries him because, in the first place, he is too old for the work he has been called to undertake and, secondly, he knows that neither his children who take him for a noisy old man nor his wife, Esther, who thinks that he is a drunkard will be inclined to agree with him. Nevertheless, he calls his favourite son, Japheth, and asks him to bring Shem for they have to build an ark before shabbos. Again, in the tradition of so many biblical prophets in the Hebrew Bible, Noah tells God that he is unworthy. With all these problems, he still cannot forget his humanity. So he asks God: "You're here yet. . . ? But wait a minute—the main point we didn't get to! You're talking a total destruction of the whole world and this is something terrible."[12] He further asks God to give a chance for the people to repent.

Japheth, though he believes in Noah's vision, does not like the idea of the Flood killing the entire humanity. He feels that one has to question such vengefulness. When Noah repeatedly tells him that he should take a wife for the new world needs "bushels of babies," Japheth is quick to ask about so many children that will be drowned in the flood. These rationalistic comments, though they speak of Japheth's commitment to man, do not convince Noah for he realizes that surely God has a purpose behind this act. On the other hand, Noah himself pleads for mercy so that they can survive.

While convincing people about the impending catastrophe if they do not repent, Noah is beaten, Japheth is almost killed and has to be saved by Goldie's intervention which proves that the evil ways of the people have gone to such an extent that God has to wipe them out and start his creation all over again. Once they are in the Ark with other animals, Japheth suggests that the Ark should be steered and hence the rudder is important. Noah rejects the idea for, he says, that God will take care of everything. They have an argument while they are at the construction of the Ark, on the issue of putting up a rudder, which forces Japheth to go away since he tries to tell Noah about its significance in vain. He comes back after a while, not because he has accepted everything, but because of his commitment to the family—for the sake of his parents and also because, without him, the Ark cannot be constructed. Here the matter of free will is given certain importance since there comes a time when Japheth has to steer the Ark to safety. For all his faith in God's providence, Noah realizes the practical aspect of the rudder and the need for human intervention in times of crisis. In fact, Japheth refuses to board the Ark as a protest against God and decides to die with other people which, he believes, affirms his sense of humanity. When he is too stubborn to take Noah's advice, Noah with the new strength given him by God, hits him hard and drags him into the Ark.

Esther is a practical Jewish housewife committed to her children and husband. She feels the burden of justifying Noah and has a moment of agony when she sees Noah in a new strength given by God. She dies before the Ark reaches the shore. Her words on the death-bed not only reflect her sense of loyalties, but also the quintessential attitude of a Jewish mother. She says that the welfare of her children is the ultimate promised land for her. On his part,

Noah experiences a process of education. From being an old man never considered highly by his children to the task of carrying God's designs, he undergoes a process of glory coupled with a personal trauma witnessing the plight of humanity. At the end of the play, Noah demands from God that there should never be another disaster, a sort of new covenant between man and God. Assured by the rainbow which is a symbol of the new covenant, he sums up his experience:

> But what I learned on the trip, dear God, you can't take it away from me.
> To walk in humility, I learned.
> And listen, even to *myself* . . . and to speak softly, with the voices of consolation. Yes, I hear You, God.
> Now it is in Man's hands to make or destroy the world—I'll tell you a mystery.[13]

These comments of Noah, together with many such comments in the play like "lonely times are not new to me,"[14] gave many critics an opportunity to read autobiographical overtones into the play. In the context of the play, Noah's words could be interpreted as something to do with his faith in God which made him plead for the survival of the people. The arduous task itself makes him a witness to the wiping out of the people with the hope of a new generation of mankind. However, the play was written at a time when so much had happened to Odets's life. His association with the left-oriented drama of which the Group Theatre became a pioneering force in the thirties and his romance with Hollywood that brought him so much of sorrow—these painful events in his life and his responses to them certainly found place in the play. Although the play is closely patterned on his aunt and uncle, the sense of remorse of McCarthyism is expressive in the drama. Odets's character and his response to the times are given to not a particular character, but are spread all over in the remarks of various characters, though mostly confined to Noah and Japheth. In this view, the play is a cathartic experience and a personal exorcism.

Odets clearly mentions in *The New York Times* article the influence of his uncle who "is very voluble, very human. It occurred to me that here was a man in flesh and blood who was the Noah of the play ... there are children and parents, with ambitions, with disappointments, with anger and love."[15] The influence of the Jewish idiom is acknowledged by Margaret Brenman-Gibson in her biography of Odets. She says: "In *The Flowering Peach*, written as Odets neared fifty, the Jewish idiom and speech melodies returned in the mouths of Noah and his wife."[16] Despite Odets's attempt at creating a true Jewish comedy in terms of contemporary American Jewish life, one critic feels that the characters look like vaudeville Jews.[17] The Jewish humour in the play unlike Miller's is a refreshing reflection of the Old Country ways of Noah and the first generation Americanized children like Japheth. In spite of various levels of interpretations, Odets's view of man, and his commitment to humanism are successfully brought out in this drama. The Jewish sensibility is implicit in every mode of it. Noah represents the old Jewish patriarch with his concern for the family. His language is that of an Old Country Jew, just emigrated to America. The mixing of Yiddish and English is a characteristic linguistic behaviour of Jewish immigrants. The Jewish rituals like shabbos and lighting Sabbath candles, the slow-rocking of Noah's prayer and the unmitigated sense of that peculiar humour which has come to be known as Jewish humour create an atmosphere of Jewish sensibility. To this end, Odets has been singularly successful. It is as if the moral aspect that haunts his plays has roots in his Jewish heritage which suddenly surfaced and synthesized in the biblical context.

Chayefsky's *Gideon* (1964) does not have any Jewish family context in the sense that has been analyzed so far. Instead, it attempts to discuss the God-man relationship, in order to come to an argument that man has not only a need to be himself, but it is necessary because without such a faith in himself, he does not find a sustaining rationale in doing what he sets out to do, whether it is under the divine grace or on his own. With this aspect as a major theme, Chayefsky recounts the life of Gideon closely on the pattern of the Yiddish play entitled *Haman's Downfall* mentioned earlier, the only variation being that in the Yiddish play the Herald reads a portion of the scroll, and the same is given dramatic situation and is enacted whereas in *Gideon*, the portion is merely mentioned and the enactment follows. Again, in *Gideon*, the Angel makes concluding remarks unlike the Herald in Haman's play.

Taken from the Book of Judges, the play deviates from the scripture and concludes in an un-biblical manner. In the demanding relationship between man and God, Chayefsky seems to emphasize the need to be human, even if it calls for acceptance of imperfection and pompousness. Starting with the idol worship of the Hebrews which displeases God, Gideon does not appear to be the biblical hero who defeated the Midiantites and saved the Hebrews from destruction. Instead, he is a *schlemiel* of the Yiddish tradition who is aptly called "a witless ass," and "a donkey" and Gideon also is aware of his foolishness. But God's Angel chooses him only to prove that it is God who has saved them from destruction and hence the need for a renewed faith in fulfilling God's covenant with Israel.

When the Angel calls Gideon a man of valour, he is scared and promptly asks his father, Joash, to deal with him. Though apparently foolish, Gideon has his own reasons for many aspects of life. He knows that his tribe is oppressed by the Midiantites and this, coupled with the agricultural fertility needs, drove them to believe in Gods and idols. But he realizes that the sacrifices offered to the idol are not eaten by any God but that only a black crow comes and feeds on it. And this crow can be driven off by Gideon. This rational thinking also makes him ask the Angel that, if the Lord is with the Hebrews, as the Angel keeps harping time and again, he finds no reason why the Hebrews should face hard times. Taking the cue, the Angel gives reasons to Gideon sitting with him like a farmer of the East. Having established a friendly relationship, the Angel asks him to be a general to fight the enemies, which he accepts reluctantly.

However, the elders of the tribe ask him to tell him about the plan at the time of war. Gideon does not have any, and so has to ask the Angel. Asked by the Angel that he should kill the Hebrews of Succoth who strayed from God's ways, Gideon cannot bring himself to kill the pitiable old men and leaves them unharmed. He pleads for the old men. Later, Gideon asks the Angel, now a victorious hero, to allow him to be the king of Israel and thus accept his vanity. The Angel rejects this plea. The Angel also observes the change in Gideon after victory. Initially it was for "the Lord and Gideon." And now that he has won the war and is screaming orders like a general, Gideon begins to enjoy this new position and changes the saying to "for Gideon and the Lord." Though Gideon likes to take the credit for the victory, he grudgingly tells the elders that the Lord was responsible for it. These aspects affirm the human side of Gideon. When he tells God that his son, Jether, does not have any respect for him, he is talking about the dignity of a father that he does not enjoy. It is, again, his commitment to man and his deeply felt sympathy that makes him ask the Lord to forgive the elderly people who are, after all, Hebrews and, therefore, must be given a chance to repent. Gideon realizes that he cannot simply be a mouthpiece of God forever, and he should have his incorrigible humanity also which, as the Lord confirms, is not possible for him if he is faithful to the Lord. He asks the Angel to relieve him from the covenant and let him be a man with all his vanity and pompousness since to love God, one has to be a God himself. He continues: "I did not kill the elders of Succoth, and I shall tell you why. I raised my spear above their heads, but in that moment I felt a shaft of terror that chills me even now. It was as if the nakedness of all things was exposed to me, and I saw myself, all men for what we truly are. . . . I cannot love you, God, for it makes me meaningless thing."[18] Finally, Gideon pleads with God to let him be his own self for the love of God. With these words and against thundering warnings of the Lord, he wears the golden ephod which is given as a present to the Lord, symbolically voicing the author's vision that from then on, man replaces God by becoming God himself, which can be interpreted in two ways: One that God is dead and hence benefitting from Renaissance humanism, man should occupy the centre stage in civilization, and second, by growing in stature of humanistic thought, man could be God and acquire divine benevolence for man. Deciding to be himself, he changes the story of the war, altogether not reiterating his previous version that the victory is due to God, but by taking recourse to his uncle Hezekiah's rationalistic interpretation of the situation. In this version the war is an inevitable growth of "historico-economic, socio-psychological and cultural forces prevailing in these regions."[19] Gideon's personality progresses from a schlemiel-figure to a man affirming not only humanity but accepting a challenge from the Angel only to remain what he is and can be, though it may cause disaster. However, there is also a possibility, in both God's and Gideon's despair, to find a certain acceptability on the part of the Lord of the new stature that has become a proverbial "man's estate." And the Angel, after all, is willing to give him a chance which is communicated in "let him don my gold ephod/ And let him be a proper God./ Well, let him try it any way."[20]

In the biblical version, Gideon has no such problem with God and happily dies at a ripe old age. Chayefsky's conclusion does not have scriptural sanction, though the author's intentions cannot be blamed for his apocryphal conclusion. Critics, as usual, responded differently. Robert Brustein, typically enough for him, says that the author combined "secular sentiments with religious pieties, vaudeville effects with Herman Wouk's metaphysics and the titillation of revolt with the security of conformity."[21] He further states that Gideon is reduced to "a lumpish mediocrity."[22] Howard Taubman's assessment is sober when he says that Gideon is some kind of Judaic Henry V and, like McLeish, Chayefsky seems to believe that instead of glorifying God, man should glorify himself[23] for withstanding the onslaught of elusive self which causes unmitigated anxiety.

Both of these views not only need a clarification but also a revision. Brustein fails to recognize that Gideon is not a mediocrity. On the contrary, he is some kind of latter-day schlemiel, which is affectionately popular in Yiddish and twentieth century Jewish literature; and it is the Jewish sensibility of the centuries of wisdom that is behind such a prototype. Pitted against the circumstances of oppression which drove them into ghettoes, the Jewish mind created such a prototype which, while glorifying the virtue of humanity and burden of sufferance, can also have the merit of deserving divine approval. Gideon, though he is a hero in the scripture, has been given this folklore image which is so common in Jewish literature.

This interpretation goes to suggest that these eminent critics, probably erred on this score, for, even the glorification of man, as Taubman asserts, can be easily analyzed in these terms. Although apparently radical, one cannot make a mistake of calling Gideon an atheist or a non-believer, for the play does not support this view. Gideon is aware that the Lord is responsible for whatever he has achieved. If he chooses to give a different version, it is only because he has to assert his humanity, in the absence of which he finds no meaning for his existence. Even so, his symbolic wearing of the ephod takes place with the remark that if God loves him, let him wear it and not cause his death. Since nothing happens to Gideon, it is safe to surmise that God certainly loves him and as the Angel's final words mark, the Lord is willing to give him a chance. Which is why one cannot call this play a radical version. In fact, one could even go to the extent of saying that Chayefsky's attempts could be understood as having a pertinent argument in domesticating the rationalistic view in theological terms. The audience is attentive to the entire gamut of history of the war and Gideon's role in it, protected by the divine will which confirms such an argument.

Howard Nemerov, an important American poet, explores the landscape of Saul's mind in *Endor* (1962). Saul without God's favour does not know what to do in trying circumstances. He comes to the witch of Endor to know his future though he forbade witchcraft and divination himself. The audience finds Saul alone, outside the witch's house. Obviously his Minister and Commander are inside, to convince her to call up the ghost of Samuel which makes Saul realize that "the king/Needs what the king forbids."[24] Saul ponders over the situation from the time when he went against the word of God by not killing the King of Amalek. Saul, overcome by pity, could not bring himself to kill the Philistine, for, he had reasoned, "What difference does one more corpse make?" He also saw fear in the king's eyes. Later Samuel slaughters the king of Amalek and anoints David, thus cursing Saul. Saul is alone at the moment and in a desperate state of mind, comes to the witch to find "my terrible peace." Outside the witch's house he beats his fist on the ground to ask Samuel's forgiveness and promises him that he would be an obedient son. But he knows that he stands alone in the world. The witch comes and is scared, for she fears that she may be killed for her art of conjuring spirits. Saul even kneels to her and tells her that she will not be hurt. The Minister and the Commander turn aside with scorn and shame at the degradation of Saul. Saul swears by the Lord God of Israel which surprises even the witch. Saul and the witch enter the House leaving the Minister and the commander to speculate on their lives and roles. The minister needs to be absolutely loyal and "a hypocrite, a sycophant, a pimp" to "serve the lusts of majesty,"[25] whereas the commander should practise "the profession of fidelity"[26] surviving the vicissitudes of the king's mind. In their wanderings of mind, the audience is acquainted with many aspects of their crisis. Saul appears to be a man of occasional temper given to melancholy and periods of suspicion. David is presently serving the king of Gath for his own ends. They also think over the idea of knowing the future and its consequences. Once the future is foretold, the Commander wonders, if discipline and obedience can be guaranteed at all. As these ruminations start flowing from their minds, Saul lets out a cry and the two courtiers enter the interior of the dwelling.

Aware of the fact that it is Saul who is present at her place, the witch gives a positive picture of the future which enrages Saul. Much against the protest of the courtier who pleads not to attempt to know the future, Saul commands the witch to start the spell. Saul also knows what is happening to him;

> When Samuel died, the voice of God fell silent
> Within me and around me, and my realm,
> Wanting in metaphysical love and truth,
> Shriveled inside.[27]

Saul falls fainting after Samuel's pronouncement of death that will take place the next day. The commander is quick to tell him that it is "a trick of the fire" which "perfected the illusion."[28] After Saul is taken inside for rest, the minister comes back to know his fate. Instead, he sees the enactment of Saul's death. Saul asks the commander to kill him since the Philistines have overcome his forces and once they find him, he may have to face a miserable death. Though initially reluctant, the commander stabs him to death and takes the crown with a hope to give it to David to gain some favour. David tells the commander that he spilled the blood of God's anointed and hence he should be killed. David composes a psalm to commemorate Saul. But the minister does not find himself at the centre of action. After a while, food is served but Saul is already affected by the knowledge of the future. He reminisces and wonders at God's ways. He could not kill the poor man in Amalek, because he looked helpless. He did not want to be a king and probably would have a quiet life like that of the witch's. The old man of God, Samuel, found him when he was looking for the stray sheep and anointed him as the King. As these memories resurface the minister announces that the commander would be killed by David harping on the hand of destiny. The puzzling aspect of the situation still puzzles him:

> He may say I was cruel to David, and
> It was for that I lost the kingdom; then
> He might say I was kind to Amalek
> And lost the kingdom for my kindness; either
> Or both become inscrutable toward the end.[29]

Saul kisses the witch affectionately after food and drink and leaves the place to face the mercy of time. The play focusses on the personality of Saul in various situations, not necessarily chosen by himself, and yet has the responsibility to face the predicament although Saul wonders why he has to be punished for being human and, being what he is, showing mercy to a fellow-human being. The play makes an attempt, and is successful in this endeavour, to present Saul as a person of humanity and hence deserves sympathy and respect for choosing to be what he is, though he surely must have thought of the consequences of the transgression of divine command. Nemerov's *Cain* (1962), another verse play, once again delves into the mind of Cain. Like Saul, Cain also fails to understand why he is not favoured by God though he has to toil throughout to bring out a good harvest. He is pained to realize that Abel's meat is accepted, whereas his vegetables and flowers are left alone. Adam and Abel are obedient and respect divine ways. Cain and Eve appear to be the questioning agents. Abel is right when he ways that Cain does not accept life as it is, though Cain protests that Abel has to kill the poor lamps. Cain does not hesitate to say that everything is left except the smoke which reflects his skepticism. Eve too complains that the "Lord's way with me/was very arbitrary."[30] Cain is asked to sit separately for they fear that something calamitous may happen. Adam reaffirms the feeling that since God does not respect Cain's offering, it is presumptuous in them to do so. That he has not done anything wrong, and is admonished all the same, troubles Cain. Cain comes up with an idea that God once did favour the garden, which is why He put Adam and Eve there. When he says that they must have done something wrong which might have changed God's mind, Adam points out that Cain's ingratitude in showing disrespect to him by blaming them is surely a fault in Cain for which he is punished. As a response to Eve's reassertion that it is their fault, Adam rationalizes their fall stating that it is, in fact, a piece of luck, for the Garden is no place to bring children up since everything is provided for them. Whatever happened to them, he says, is the will of God. Cain speculates on the moment of fright before death which may force man to kill, knowing that there is no where to run to escape death. This understanding of Cain foretells what is to happen later in his life when he is to kill Abel "seeing he cannot save himself."[31] In a dialogue between Cain and God, the former asks as to why the things are as they are. When Cain asks initially the reasons for preferring Abel's offering and hence Abel himself, God's voice tells him that Cain is avoiding the real question he wants to ask. The voice also tells him that if he does well, his offering will also be accepted and warns him that sin is always lurking round the corner. God further explains:

Things are as they are
Until you decide to change them,
But do not be surprised if afterward
Things are as they are again.[32]

While aptly emphasizing the role of human intervention in history, the view also underlines the fact that sometimes even these changes may not bring the desired alteration. With these remarks, He also tells Cain that there is nothing that can prevent him from ruling over Abel which Cain interprets according to his own convenience and kills Abel. Since Abel is loved by God, Cain believes that here is a sacrifice from Cain which will be favoured by God—an "acceptable sacrifice."[33] God asks him if this act is good or bad for which Cain does not have any answer except that he understands that "a man may be the master here"[34]—not Abel who is killed, but Cain is the master. He is also reminded of the fact his parents may kill him and, therefore, should run away with the saving mark of God. Cain is "one/of my holy ones" from whose discovery great cities of men will be built. Posterity, Cain is told, will remember him as a person who has found things as they are and changed them and yet found them still the same. Cain questions why all these things should happen at all for which God answers metaphorically that He is the serpent in the Garden. He warns him that though he wants to reject God, Cain cannot do this. These happenings are part of his education which brings him to a realization that man cannot change things back which "may be the only change worth having."[36] Cain leaves and Adam and Eve once again think about what they have to do. Adam says that they should reconsider the past and go to the gate of the Garden and ask God either to take them in or kill them. Adam wonders if they have to take "the terrible night into ourselves"[37] and make a morning of it. With these words of repentance and unavoidable courage, they determine to live together till "death or day light."[38]

Adam and Eve are left alone waiting for old age and death. The play, for all its biblical spirit, though interpreted in Nemerov's viewpoint, still makes one wonder why Abel, for no fault of his, should be killed and Cain, having killed Abel even with a hope to change things, is the holy one of God with His protective mark. It may probably mean that the free will of Cain, with whatever consequences, is possibly endearing himself to God, though Cain, like Adam and Eve, has abused his freedom to choose and act. Cain cannot answer if the killing of Abel is good or bad—this ethical perspective hardly touches his mind. Knowing that his offering is not accepted, he gives the only offering that could find favour in God's eyes. This yearning to be accepted by God coupled with an urge to change things, though he almost immediately realizes that nothing has changed, is redeeming, for, as God says, from this urge and aspiration can the great cities and monuments be created, notwithstanding the fact that some of them in due course of time may be disastrous to humanity. This, once again, depends on the efficacy of man's ethical vision. Maimonides, a revered interpreter of the scripture, points out that Adam and Eve have been given intellect which can only distinguish between the truth and falsehood. However, it is only after the Fall that they could realize the ethical side of everything, for, Maimonides believes, that the ethical view largely depends on general agreement. This ethical view possibly is what makes them feel ashamed when they suddenly realize that they are naked.[39] Both of Nemerov's plays, while delving into essential theological arguments, also present these biblical figures as human beings in situations which demand so much from them. Saul in *Endor* desperately looks for an alternative structure of defence and security in the absence of divine favour and Cain, haunted by the fact that he is not favoured, takes to an unethical course of action though it may have a constructive consequence. These characters, along with many such figures in the dramatic presentation of the biblical episodes, are forced into situations for which they are not entirely responsible; and if they are, as in Saul's case, it is within the realm of their human fallibility. But they are to grapple with reality and find a solution and a redemptive meaning.

Man's predicament to face the most trying situation is, once again, presented in Joel Schwartz's *Two Psalms of David* (1972) which depicts two periods in David's life: one as an entertainer in Saul's court and second, as a king. The play takes a liberal view of the biblical context and gives a new orientation to it by introducing a political aspect. Hence the first section concentrates on the inter-tribal conflict: the tribe of Judah represented by David having a problem in the Benjamite court of Saul. Initially, Saul is not tempted and, in fact, treats David as his own son. Immensely affectionate though Saul is towards David, he feels threatened the moment he senses that David is liked by all and the people are glorifying his name in preference to Saul's. Already aware that God is not with him, which possibly is the reason for his moods and erratic behaviour, David's popularity pains him singularly. So he conceives a strategy as a part of which David is to marry his daughter, Michal, which should assure him the required security. This action is only tentative and later he realizes that David should be killed since there is always a possibility of danger. Informed by Jonathan about Saul's plan, David flees. David protests when Samuel, the prophet, says that he should be the next king under the assumption that Saul is like a father to him and, in any case, how can one be sure that God approves of this. Then Samuel shows what is to happen, in a mystical manner, to Saul and Jonathan. In the second act, David faces a different crisis, this time it is not the inter-tribal conflict but the conflict within the family. David, now the king of Israel, does everything he wants and builds a dwelling place for the Ark and establishes the kingdom of peace until Ammon rapes his half-sister, Tamar. Absalom takes revenge by killing Ammon and sets up his own supporters, advised by Achitophel to lead a war against David. David, a loving father, does not like bloodshed in Jerusalem, the city of God. He is also receptive to the fact that Achitophel is popular. David lives the role of Saul. David leaves the city to Absalom and goes into hiding. Absalom takes over the kingdom but Achitophel is wary and tells him that Absalom should take the harem left behind by David and also wage war against David, for they cannot rest as long as David is alive. Although David shows his paternal affection for his son by admonishing his soldiers not to kill him, cruel fate overtakes him when Absalom's hair is caught in the branches of a tree while he was galloping. Saul's death and Absalom's death complete the cycle of agony of David which makes him wonder why he always has to fight the people he loves dearly. He composes a poem on Saul's death. And this time the 'figure' of King David tells him to take the advice of Samuel and states that the only way of serving God is to use one's own free will. Had he taken immediate action against Haman, this tragedy would not have occurred just as, had Saul obeyed the command, his reign would have continued. And the play ends with an affirmation in God's ways with due emphasis on man's free will and right choices.

These arguments probably are not substantiated in the scriptures. This is what prompted the author to suggest that "the production should in no way suggest a biblical context."[40] Besides, the play is significant in its masterly use of technique and presentation. Thus, the mime technique, slow motion, flashback, tableau, are used effectively in tune with the theme of the play. The actors read the libretto in philharmonic fashion and quickly join other actors, once they complete reading it, to take their position for different roles. This is used to suggest especially the battle scenes. The passage of time is suggested through chanting the months of the Hebrew calendar. Saul's death is mourned on stage when they recite the Jewish prayer for the dead—Kaddish.

Once again the plight of making unwilling choices falls on not only both Saul and David but also on Absalom. Whatever be the political situation that serves as a backdrop, Saul, loving David as a son, cannot ignore the fact that in the absence of external favour, if he has to preserve his existence as a king, he has to think in terms of vanquishing David. This does not underscore their mutual affection. Similarly, David's love for Absalom does not stop an inevitable battle though, understandably, Achitophel's advice to Absalom is as practical as any political decision would be. However, the latter hesitates a little since he has to fight against his own father; David's lapse in leaving Ammon unpunished for his treacherous act eclipses him. Here again, we see them taking unavoidable recourse to actions necessitated by certain circumstances beyond them.

Barrie Stavis's *Coat of Many Colors* (1968) reflects the perennial struggle waged by the biblical Joseph against the unscrupulous external forces in order to change them hoping to establish peace and prosperity. Always a dreamer among his brethren, he leads a crisis-ridden life for his dreams. Not content with the things as they are and believing that Jehovah as a purpose which is to be fulfilled through him, he dreams of adventure and attempts to change external circumstances for the benefit of humanity. This does not prevent him from encountering another type of danger presented to him through self-serving and self-perpetuating institutions though these institutions nurture themselves on the unchanging poverty and passivity of the people.

Sold over and over again, first by his own brothers and later by other slave-traders, Joseph refuses to learn the fact that it is precisely his interference with the passive system that causes trouble for him. He is repeatedly thrown into pit but he never gives up. He virtually runs Egypt for two years as incognito ruler assisting Potiphar. When he makes bold designs to bring permanent prosperity and peace to Egypt, Vashnee, wife of Potiphar, protests. He wants to build dams on the Nile and channelize water for permanent irrigation which may prevent starvation of the people. By doing that, he is destroying the rights and powers of the priesthood which controls the sacred waters and believes that the prosperity and famine are divine matters not to be meddled with by humans. Despite his problems, Joseph resurfaces to prominence through his ingenuity and smartness with the approval of the Pharaoh but miscalculates the effect of such hard work on the engineers and workers who prefer an easy life of passivity. Put to continuous work, they grumble and this is promptly taken advantage of by his opponents. Although Joseph tries to convince them, his suggestions fall on deaf ears. Serving a rebellious mob, drudgery which surely guarantees his power. Later Vashnee and the Pharaoh send him to the desert, which means retirement, with Vashnee asking his servants to kill him. From being a dreamy boy of Jacob to a man who dares to put his dreams into practice, it is a long journey. Though his fate is pitiable at the end of the play, it is because of him that the granaries are built. If his confidence is a sign of his survival from the danger of Vashnee's conspiracy, he may well come back and complete his project. As the play comes to an end, the Pharaoh shrinks into a mummy just as Vashnee turns into a statue which suggests that these people remain merely actors of history, of personal convenience, whereas Joseph's faith in free will and man's intervention in history in the form of whatever changes he brought, stand as a testimony to his faith in human improvement. Joseph realizes that he failed to understand the fact that he cannot put the people to endless work which probably made them feel like slaves, and hence looked for liberation. This attitude helped the designs of the priesthood and Vashnee. Joseph tells the Pharoah that the time is not ripe for him to tell the people of the falseness of the priesthood and "if that time ever comes, the gods and their superstitions, the tyrants and their slavery will vanish. For these men will be heroes, and heroes need no gods and no tyrants."[41]

In terms of dramaturgy, Reuben acts as a narrator, a sort of choric figure, who informs us about the intervening times and events. The author interferes with the biblical episode once when Vashnee entices Joseph in a bid to make him abandon his project of the dams in favour of granaries to store food at the time of good harvest. Joseph, falling a prey to this pretension, kisses her. The author introduces the correct version immediately since Reuben reads the biblical version which is enacted subsequently. Commenting upon the character of Joseph, John Lewin in his introduction, writes: "He must take advantage of the cynicism of the Pharaoh and Vashnee by outshining them with his own shrewdness; hence to an extent he may strike the superficial observer, unaware of what it means for a displaced person to survive in a hostile land, as the prototype of the Clever Jew."[42] At least once his shrewdness and urge to dominate and rule over others is flatly rejected when Reuben along with his brothers, comes to Egypt to take food-stuffs and, incidentally, realizes that the ruler is none other than their own brother. Reuben prefers to side with his brothers now, though he pleaded in his favour when Joseph was to be sold, by stating that he cannot condone Joseph's views. As a narrator, he also rightly sums up that Joseph goes on learning and the process of education continues while appreciating his achievements as a reformer.

Neil Simon's *God's Favourite* (1974) is not exactly a biblical play, though the characters are patterned on the Scripture. It is a story of a contemporary business man, Joe Benjamin, who is based on Job. In a strenuous debate between God and Lucifer, it falls to the lot of God to prove that there is at least one man in the world who does not renounce Him whatever be the hardship he is to face. This should have been a serious theological and philosophical subject matter as it surely is in Archibald McLeish's Pulitzer Prize-winning *J.B.* (1956). Neil Simon makes a lively comedy out of the biblical story which is unanimously approved by the New York critics who, as the saying goes, can make or break the plays. Joe Benjamin is a wealthy man but he gives half of his profits to charity. David, his son, resents their excessive wealth and takes to alcoholism though Joe tells him that he is not responsible for their wealth and hence is god-given. Neil Simon mentions in the stage directions that it is today, "and yet it has a feeling of a timelessness"[42] and thus hints at the biblical resonances in the play. Joe is a man of character and David's behaviour pains him. Sidney Lipton, the messenger of God, tells him that he has a word from God to Joe which does not impress him that much and, for all his knowledge, Sidney may be a fool himself. After a series of effective, if comical and esoteric, conversations he realizes that Sidney has a purpose in his visit, though he is worried that his wife, Rose, may get excited at the prospect of the events to follow. Sidney tells him that he is God's favourite and is to be tested for what he is. Joe faces the loss of his industry and virtual poverty with a moral strength and still does not stray away from his faith. David is not convinced with his logic and thinks that he should settle matters in a court regarding Sydney. He even protests against God which is answered with a fierce lightning. Later, David loses his eyesight for his skepticism which proves to be the last straw for Joe. He quarrels with God by questioning His sense of justice and compassion. He asks Him to take revenge against him and spare his son. Despite these quarrels with God, he affirms that he still believes in Him. Once the test is complete David recovers his eyesight and things begin to improve financially. David regains his faith and Sidney, at the end of the play, once again, tells him the same words he did to his father, implying that David, like his father, has to undergo the travails of God's test.

Although this is what happens in the play thematically, the real significance lies in the effective comedy Simon weaves from the available subject matter. Working in the long tradition of Jewish American comedy spanning over a long period from David Belasco and the immigrant Yiddish-English comedy through Kaufman and Hart, S.N. Behrman and recently Jules Feiffer, Woody Allen, Bruce Jay Friedman and a score of others, Simon generally expands a schema of comic atmosphere to an otherwise fairly serious human problems as can be seen in *Sunshine Boys* (1972), *The Odd Couple* (1965), *Chapter Two* (1977) and *Brighton Beach Memoir* (1984) to name only a few. Edythe McGovern rightly points out that "his plays which may appear simple to those who never look beyond the fact that they are amusing one, in fact, frequently more perceptive and revealing of the human condition than many plays labelled complex dramas."[44] Interestingly so, the great psychoanalysts like Sigmund Freud and Theodor Reik paid attention to Jewish humour. Reik in his book entitled *Jewish Wit* (1962) states that "Jewish jokes often reveal those hidden sides of truth."[45] Neil Simon's Jewish comedy, as has been mentioned already, certainly conforms to this view.

The comic aspect in these biblical plays, while extending the aspect of humour in Jewish literature, also serves as an intensive force to the themes they strive to explicate. Thus, Arthur Miller, Clifford Odets and Neil Simon have used the comic aspect to a great extent while it is minimal in other playwrights. In many of these plays, the protagonists are patterned as modified schlemiel-figures of Jewish tradition. Noah, Adam and Joe in the plays of Odets, Miller and Simon respectively fit into the category of the schlemiel-figure, though they are much larger than this category, and function in a wider canvas to be representatives of the avowed themes of their authors. Even Gideon, in Chayefsky's play, functions as a traditional schlemiel fulfilling the qualities of a luckless person though, unlike other counterparts of the tradition, he benefits from the divine favour and becomes a hero. Ruth Wisse commenting on the image of the schlemiel in modern Jewish writing focuses on its suggestiveness: "The generations of Jews who lived as God's people, sanctifying every act of private and communal life in accordance with their understanding of His commandments, considered all afflictions as rebukes in His ongoing efforts to forge a righteous man."[46] The image of schlemiel encompasses the perpetual afflictions as a category of his life. This view partly explains the treatment of the schlemiel even in the biblical episodes. As is mentioned already, the schlemiel version in their plays is not traditional since these schlemiels, though foolish and luckless initially, grow in stature due to divine presence and, therefore, reach heroic proportions by occupying a position as God's favourities. Biblical episodes have been variously used by Jewish playwrights. Some of them created Jewish family situations with an essential commentary on the spiritual dimension. They have also drawn enormously from the classical Yiddish literature. Others like Odets found a therapeutic possibility in identifying themselves with the biblical characters sharing the anguish of being men of their personal experience with similar characters in the Bible. But it is the genius of the Jewish playwrights that has been responsible for viable and sustaining situations which conforms to the spirit of the scriptures. For Chayefsky, Nemerov and Schwartz it is a dialogue between man and God. Nemerov and Schwartz attempt to understand the psyche of the people who do not know why such a predicament falls on them. Their sense of humanity also warns the contemporary man that while it is difficult being a divine favourite, it is pernicious not to be a man. The dilemma of these choices—there does not seem to be any choice in the case of both Saul and David—leads man to a journey which is tortuous though, in the last assessment, it may be spiritually ennobling. The Humanistic vision in the Hebraic scriptures is not only domesticated to the contemporary reality but also interpreted in the Jewish tradition which makes these works supremely fascinating. And the humour, apart from the family situations, while presenting the themes in a lively manner also points out even by an ordinary theatre goer. This element of humour is either minimal as in Archibald Mc Leish's *J.B.* (1956) and *Nobodaddy* (1926) or has been given folk-dimension as in Marc Connelly's *The Green Pastures* (1930). Besides the theological differences, these plays also cry out for a need to be human and cherish concern for our other less fortunate brethren. Mc Leish's *J.B.* in fact, has a searing debate on inscrutable divine ways and man's need to know why he is as he is. J.B.'s wife, Sarah, questions his faith in God to such an extent that he can rationalize not only their misfortune but also the death of his children:

> They are
> Dead and they were innocent: I will not
> Let you sacrifice their deaths,
> To make injustice justice and God good.[47]

At the close of the play, J.B. too asks questions and, guided by his wife, chooses to be a man, for there is no justice and there is only the world we live in and love. Hence they are determined to blow "on the coal of the heart."[48] Mc Leish's Pulitzer-winning play highlights the crisis of the modern man and the injustice that becomes such an unavoidable truth and hence the skepticism that seeks divine justification for such a reality just as Cain in *Nobodaddy* surmises that having killed Abel, he "has become a man."[49] Zuss and Nickles, in *J.B.*, are circus vendors, who wear the masks of God and Satan to play their role. In the process, they seem to live the roles they are to act true to the philosophy of the Strasberg Actors Studio which was influenced to a large extent by Stainslavsky. They also speak of similar contexts in modern life. *The Green Pastures* tells the biblical tale with a Negro cast using the Negro dialect and has the form of a miracle play. Also a Pulitzer-winner, it has a message of mutual tolerance and fellow feeling:

> The "religious truths" of the play are not, however, concerned with a question of theology. It is, rather, concerned

> with man's relationship to man. If, the play seems to ask, even with a just God, man sins but is yet redeemed because he knows suffering and has learned mercy, how should men treat each other? Specifically, the question raised for an American audience centers around the attitude for fortunate white-American theatre-goers should have towards "the less fortunate of these, thy brothers."[50]

The theological plays of Mc Leish and Marc Connelly are at variance with the Judaic viewpoint especially their views on the Fall, guilt, mercy, suffering and redemption. However, their treatment of the themes, with its relevance to the present social set-up is exemplary in the sense that though the technique and situations of their plays do not have the same degree of scope which one finds in the Jewish plays, their humanistic vision is compelling. The foremost reason for this is the essential concern for man and the relationship between man and God which becomes the rock-bed of the Hebraic sources themselves. For some people like Joel Schwartz and Barrie Stavis, the episodes in the Bible become useful myths to be utilized for contemporary contexts. Thus, Schwartz makes it a point to mention specifically that a deliberate attempt should be made to avoid the biblical context. Similarly, Barrie Stavis even revises the story of Joseph but holds himself and introduces a choric device which rectifies the revision in order to give the impression to the audience that his revision is probable but the original context is authentic. His vision in the play that man can achieve anything if he acts courageously to put into practice what he desires through rationalistic assessment of the situation, may be justifiable cause that prompted him to venture a revision. Although the Jewish playwrights are tremendously successful in weaving a recognizably enduring situation from the limited description of the sources, they also take precaution not to digress from the essence and spirit of the context which, in itself, is guided by the knowledge and understanding of the sustaining sources like the scriptures, the Talmud and other interpretations of Rabbinic Judaism. This, however, should not give the impression that these playwrights have a regular Yeshiva upbringing. But they are receptive to the various currents in Jewish history which secular Jewish literature of modern times reflected. Further, classical Yiddish literature captures the nationalist fervour of *galut* while authentically finding meaningful prototypes in the Hebrew Bible. Thus even the apparent biblical episode unmistakably communicates views to suit the contemporary situation. With the Jewish assimilation and integration, though the "melting pot" is abandoned in favour of cultural pluralism, the tradition of relevance of the biblical contexts to the present day continues. But this time, their treatment includes wider experience, often encompassing the vision of universalism as has been shown in the preceding arguments of the plays. Inevitably, the literary endeavour of the Jewish creative efforts bear a lasting testimony to the crisis of the times with a statement of the growing need for everyone to be an apostle of humanism.

NOTES

1. Elie Wisel, "A Personal Response," *Face to Face: An Interreligious Bulletin*, 6 (1979), p. 37.
2. Chaim Sloves, *Haman's Downfall, Epic and Folk Plays of Yiddish Theatre*, ed. and trans. David Lifson (Madison: Fairleigh Dickinson Univ. Press, 1975).
3. Arthur Miller, *Creation of the World and Other Business* (New York: Viking Press, 1972), p. 7.
4. *Ibid.*, p. 19.
5. *Ibid.*, p. 18.
6. *Ibid.*, p. 38.
7. *Ibid.*, p. 106.
8. Daniel Walden, "Miller's Roots and His Moral Dilemma: or, Continuity from Brooklyn to *Salesman*," *Critical Essays on Arthur Miller*, James J. Martine, ed. (Boston: G.K. Hall, 1979), p. 195.
9. Robert Gordis, *Judaism for the Modern Age* (New York: Farrar, 1935), p. 225.
10. Richard Watts, "Arthur Miller's *Creation* Opens at Shubert Theatre," *Critical Essays on Arthur Miller*, p. 174.

11. Stanley Kauffmann, *Persons of the Drama* (New York: Harper and Row, 1967, 1976), pp. 232-33.
12. Clifford Odets, *The Flowering Peach*, from a production copy available at the ASRC, Hyderabad, p. 9.
13. *Ibid.*, p. 117.
14. *Ibid.*, p. 7.
15. Herbert Mitgang, "Odets Goes to Genesis," *New York Times*, II (26 December, 1954), p. 1.
16. Margaret Brenman-Gibson, *Clifford Odets* (New York: Atheneum, 1982), p. 660.
17. Gerald Weales, *Clifford Odets: Playwright* (New York: Pegasus, 1971), p. 174.
18. Paddy Chayefsky, *Gideon* (New York: Random House, 1961, 1962), pp. 127-28.
19. *Ibid.*, p. 137.
20. *Ibid.*, p. 138.
21. Robert Brustein. "All Hail, Mahomet of Middle Seriousness," *New Republic*, Vol. 145 (Nov.27, 1961), p. 21.
22. *Ibid.*
23. Howard Taubman, "A Proper God," *Time* (Nov. 17, 1961), p. 71.
24. Howard Nemerov, *Endor, The Collected Poems* (Chicago: The University of Chicago Press, 1977), p. 279.
25. *Ibid.*, p. 282.
26. *Ibid.*, p. 283.
27. *Ibid.*, p. 290.
28. *Ibid.*, p. 293.
29. *Ibid.*, p. 312.
30. Howard Nemerov, *Cain, The Next Room of the Dream* (Chicago: The University of Chicago Press, 1962), p. 124.
31. *Ibid.*, p. 129.
32. *Ibid.*, p. 132.
33. *Ibid.*, p. 134.
34. *Ibid.*
35. *Ibid.*, p. 136.
36. *Ibid.*, p. 141.
37. *Ibid.*, p. 143.
38. *Ibid.*
39. Moses Maimonides, *Guide of the Perplexed* (London: East and West Library, 1972), pp. 54-55.
40. Joel Schwartz., *The Two Psalms of David from Playwrights for*

Tomorrow (Minneapolis: The University of Minnesota Press, 1972), p. 118.

41. Barrie Stavis, *Coat of Many Colors* (New York: A.S. Barnes, 1968) p. 141.
42. John Lewin, in his introduction to *Coat of Many Colors,* p. 13.
43. Neil Simon, *God's Favourite* (New York: Random House, 1975), p. 3.
44. Edythe M. McGovern, *Neil Simon: A Critical Study* (New York: Frederick Unger, 1978, rpt. 1979), p. 102.
45. Theodor Reik, *Jewish Wit* (New York: Camut Press, 1962), p. 19.
46. Ruth Wisse, *The Schlemiel as Modern Hero* (Chicago: The University of Chicago Press, 1971), p. 5.
47. Archibald Mc Leish, *J.B*. Boston: The Riverside Press, 1956, 1958), p. 110.
48. *Ibid.*, p. 153.
49. Archibald Mc Leish, *Cain, Six Plays* (Boston: Houghton Mifflin Company, 1980), p. 130.
50. Paul T. Nolan, *Marc Connelly* (New York: Twayne, 1969), p. 86.

Conclusion
Out of the Ghetto: A View from the Mainstream

The decline, if not the total disappearance, of the Jewish stereotypes not only in American literature but also in European literature is due to two main reasons. The first is a consistent effort on the part of the Jews of all walks of life to attack in every possible way the notorious prejudices that the stereotypes epitomize. Secondly, the liberal milieu created by the Enlightenment gave an unprecedented opportunity for the emergence of the Jews. Consequently, the Jewish writer found himself in an environment of positive reception which, while facilitating an interaction between Jew and gentile, also dictated a compulsion to liberate himself from the constraints of the traditional stereotype. Liberal thought, which is a child of the Age of Reason, became a driving force for many a sympathetic reappraisal of the Jewish question. This eventually paved the way for the self-conscious endeavour of the Jewish writer with a limited readership, to inch his way towards a realization of the possibility of becoming a major voice in a gentile society. In America, this transition has been realized with signal success. The immigrants of the early part of the century eagerly accepted the blessings of the "melting pot." Already familiar with the Jewish tradition of learning, the child of the Jewish immigrants performed competitively and efficiently in American schools as testified to in Nathan Glazer's *American Judaism*. At home Yiddish of the Old Country and in the schools the native language provided a composite culture which, instead of becoming a stumbling block in various ways, prepared him for an eclectic role. His subsequent contribution not only to the American language—the Yiddish and the Hebrew words and inflexions have later been accepted even by the standard lexicographers—but to belles-lettres itself is a natural consequence. The economic strength and the importance of scholastic achievement of the Jews ultimately caused their entry into the mainstream of American society.

This phase is faithfully reflected in Jewish American literature of the twenties and the thirties in the works of Abraham Cahan, Daniel Fuchs, Henry Roth, Meyer Levin and Ludwig Lewisohn—to name only a few. In their works, one perceives the typical Yiddish accidence and syntax. Their themes, however, have been usual contexts of Jewish life centred on the family with the background of a cultural clash between the ghetto life and the American social scene—the acceptance of which these immigrants desperately sought. These themes provided a schema of myriad literary possibilities. The Great Slump was the watershed which hastened Jewish integration into American society. The Jewish concern for social justice, together with the rankling sense of centuries of persecution, gave a fresh vantage point to view the American disaster from an angle that clearly bestowed upon them the much needed communication with the gentile society. It is a definitive change for, from then on, they represented not merely the Jewish point of view but the rage and concern of America itself. Mike Gold, Joseph Freeman, the Group Theatre, Clifford Odets, Granville Hicks sum up the history of the thirties. For the first time, Jews played a major role in American society and culture. The trend continues unabated till today despite certain trammels during the period of German Nazism. As early as 1939, Joseph Mersand had these comments to make: "The evaluation of the contributions of Jewish creative artist to the pre-eminence of the American drama in the world today is a hazardous undertaking. Those professional anti-Semites who will not endure the participation of the Jews in any activity denied to them in the Dark Ages will find more material for the prejudices in the statements about outstanding Jews of the American theatre. Those who are less violent in their attitude toward Jews, but who suffer from excessive xenophobia, will find such cause for regrets and laments in the fact that significant figures in the American theatre should be Jews."[1]

Having recognized the fact that the Jewish dramatists had dominated the scene in the thirties, Mersand also fears that their predominance might cause a new spate of anti-Semitism. He is only familiar with the knowledge of Jewish history that whenever a nation faces a crisis, the Jews are generally blamed as the culprits responsible for it. In the late thirties the Nazi persecution of Jews came to the knowledge of the world which inspired Mersand to make these comments. Nevertheless, the Jewish writer, in due course of time, has become a major voice of American society and quickly played the role of being a prophet of secular humanism by preaching a social gospel[2] of universal brotherhood and social justice. Any political or social system or ideology that failed to live upto the messianic dream was attacked ruthlessly. The modified and merely materialist version of the American dream, the failure of liberalism, the perversity of the Holocaust and the human predicament in the biblical plays inspire their creative work in the following decades as has been shown in the preceding chapters. In the thirties, the Jewish writer was *the* representative of the American disenchantment with the existing system. Jewish American literature, at that time, was surely in the process of coming of age. So much so, the *Contemporary Jewish Record*, the forerunner of *Commentary* asked some of the emerging Jewish writers in 1944 to express their views on how their being Jewish determines their work, especially against the background of the all-pervasive anti-Semitism. Among them were Lionel Trilling, Muriel Ruskeyser, Delmore Schwartz, Alfred Kazin and Isaac Rosenfeld. Many of them treated this idea with indifference and even with a sense of disdain while Delmore Schwartz and Isaac Rosenfeld either affirmed their Jewishness or found a useful schemata in the Jewish context that might be used as an archetype for the modern situation. Trilling stated that modern Jewish religion did not produce a singly voice "of philosophical, or poetic, or even rhetorical, let alone of religious, authority."[3] He further commented that the American Jewish Community of the time could not provide sustenance for an artist or an intellectual who was born a Jew. In his concluding remarks, he reasserts his case that he knows "no Jewish writer in English who has added a micromillimetre to his stature by 'realizing his Jewishness,' although I know of some who have curtailed their promise by trying to heighten their Jewish consciousness."[4] Kazin feels that the Jewish critics, philosophers, and social thinkers fared better than their counterparts in art and literature. Significantly, Trilling raises an interesting point when he says that some Jewish writers with their excessive concern for Jewish consciousness destroyed their potential talents. It is possible that he has writers like Ludwig Lewisohn in mind. Superimposing Jewish sensibility on the apparently non-conducive context may prove to be a discordant factor. At the same time, ignoring and deliberately trying to avoid Jewishness when it could be used profitably in creative writing takes one to another extreme point. To this extent, Trilling perhaps is writing under the stress of his time, though his comments do suggest some useful perspectives on the Jewish context. Much later in his career, Trilling outlived his views and found rabbinical overtones in Wordsworth's poetry. His article entitled "Wordsworth and the Rabbis"[5] is an excellent piece of comparative literary analysis. He also wrote an extensive article on the changing myth of Jew in English literature.[6] For Rosenfeld, another contributor to the aforementioned "Under Forty" symposium of the *Contemporary Jewish Record*, the situation of the Jew is prototypical since the dialectic of his alienation should favourably suit the modern temper. The anguish of alienation which has been a perennial fountainhead of Jewish history has its positive bearings too. Schooled in adversity, Jews recognized the need for a good society where social justice and moral vision can guarantee mutual tolerance and fellowship of man:

> But alienation from society, like the paradox of the outsider, may function as a condition of entrance into society. . . . No man suffers injustice without learning, vaguely but surely what justice is. The desire for justice, once it passes beyond revenge becomes the deepest motive for social change. Out of their recent sufferings one may expect the Jewish writer to

> make certain inevitable moral discoveries. These discoveries, enough to indict the world, may also be crucial to its salvation.[7]

The "modern temper" in Rosenfeld's thought eventually took him close to Wilhelm Reich's philosophy just as Delmore Schwartz's did. While one can appreciate the logic of Rosenfeld in drawing a parallel between the Jewish predicament of the diaspora and the "modern temper" under stress one should not confuse his paradigmatic view with the necessity of the Jewish sensibility in American Jewish writing itself. He seems to give an impression that he accepts Jewishness to the extent that it nourishes the archetype of the modern *weltenshaung*. Harold Ribalow is right when he says that these Jewish writers responded to the questionnaire with "disdain, sometimes with superior, snobbish aloofness, and by some with frank and unconcealed contempt,"[8] though for some Jewishness is an acknowledged source of inspiration and heritage.

In the mid-fifties the theme was revived by *Congress Weekly*. It chose nine Jewish novelists, which included Charles Angoff and Herman Wouk, and asked them why they had written Jewish novels and if they were happy with the response their books had received. This time there was neither irreverence nor rejection on the part of the Jewish writers. Instead, they seem to be at home with the themes and most of them expressed that the Jewish context in their works was an inevitable choice since they were familiar with it. Herman Wouk affirms that he would use the Jewish theme again in his forthcoming novels.[9] The change in the attitude and perception is positive not merely in terms of affirmation of their Jewishness but also because it is a convenient means of communication for the children of the immigrants to use it in their creative work. Inevitably, writing about a situation which is basically unfamiliar requires visualization which may not be a safer ground for an artistic success. The writer earns it from second-hand experience which does not give the required freedom to use it effectively in the creative process.

The fascination with the Jewish sensibility in Jewish writing was to continue to occupy the minds of Jewish scholars. In the 1961 April issue of *Commentary,* there appeared the response of young Jewish writers to a topic entitled "Jewishness and the Young Intellectuals." Philip Roth believed that the increasing assimilation of the Jewry and the disappearance of anti-Semitism in America would make it possible for a man to choose to be a Jew and not turned into one by a hostile society. For John Hollander, a poet has different issues to grapple with. As a poet, even if Jewish, he has to concern himself with "language and form, style and rhetoric" while Irving Feldman recognizes "*messiahship* in which each Jew must imitate the patriarchs and prophets, in which he is responsible not only for the deliverance of the Jews but also for the perfection of the world."[10] These two poets have certainly tried to identify the usable past in their poetry which should please critics like Harold Bloom who found fault with the emerging Jewish poets for their lapse in not projecting Jewishness for a profitable execution of themes and techniques. However, as Podhoretz rightly suggests, these writers neither reject their heritage nor do they rush enthusiastically towards it. They showed displeasure at the middle-classness of Jews but "by committing themselves to the Ideal in culture and politics, they were being more truly Jewish than the community which called itself Jewish."[11]

Almost a quarter-century later, the Jewishness of the Jewish writer is still a favourite issue especially for academic arguments. The Jewish writer however, has been depicting Jews and Jewish contexts in his works in the recent years. Later on, most of them—this includes Saul Bellow, Bernard Malamud and Philip Roth—did not want to be classified as "Jewish American Writer." This attitude, however, should not be confused with a rejection of Jewishness. They seem to fear that the overtones of parochialism of such a term may belie their fervent universalism. Otherwise, their works attempt to deal with the situation of Jews, oftentimes semiconsciously choosing the subject matter. Writers like Chaim Potok, Malamud, Cynthia Ozick—to name just a few—consciously weave an authentic synthesis of the modern Jewish experience and the Jewish tradition in order to arrive at universal themes. The fact that these Jewish writers are representative literary voices, despite their varying emphasis on ethnicity, proves the universality of their act. Since this is the state of affairs, they show reluctance at accepting "Jewish American Writer" as a practical term. Asked by a team of interviewers how he reacts to a general tendency on the part of the Jewish scholars and academics to categorize them as part of Jewish American literature, Malamud states that the "term is schematic and reductive. If the scholar needs the term he can use it, but it won't be doing him any good if he limits his interpretation of a writer to fit a label he applies."[12] Abraham Rothberg believes that the term "Jewish writer" is a linguistic convenience focussing issues related to "the Jew as well as . . . the writer, not to speak of that combined and different entity, 'the Jewish writer'."[13] Even as the discussion on the Jewish writer continues, Podhoretz asserts that the Jewish writer should come to terms with the tradition and transform his heritage into a recognizable fact in art. Harold Bloom in his book entitled *Figures Capable of Imagination* restates what Podhoretz said in 1961. While commenting on the situation of American Jewish poetry, he wonders why there are no preeminent poets of frontline status on a par with novelists like Bellow, Malamud, and Roth. He seems to be cheerful, however, at the emergence of poets like Hollander, Feldman and some new voices who, according to him, are in the right direction, instead of being burdened by the legacy of modernist or post-modernist *angst*. He writes:

> There is no recovery of covenant of the Law, without confronting again, in all deep tribulation, the God of the Fathers, who is beyond image as He is beyond personality, and who can be met only by somehow again walking His way. For all our mutual skepticisms, the increasing enterprise of American Jewish poetry is what it should be: persistence in seeking to recover what our ancestors had.[14]

From indifference and tolerance to a vigorous affirmation of Jewishness and the Jewish heritage—which make up the structure of Jewish consciousness, even if it is given a secularized stance—the Jewish writer seems to have graduated to his advantage. Although Bloom writes about the newly energized American Jewish poetry and its positive trend, the Jewish sensibility is more authentic in other genres. The novelists like Potok and Ozick consciously tried to create believable situations in their tradition which became acceptable and are widely read even by the gentiles. The subject matter of Jews and Jewishness has achieved a status of a marketable commodity. So much so, some of the best seller virtuosoes like Leon Uris, James A. Michener, Irving Wallace, Lawrence Sanders, Robert Ludlum, Harold Robbins, Cynthia Freeman, Sidney Sheldon and a score of others wrote about the Jewish experience. Herbert Gold, Howard Faust and Irvin Shaw wrote, and some continue to write, what is called middle-brow fiction bringing Jewish context frequently into their work. These writers, and certainly many more, are not merely Jewish writers in America. Their increasing popularity—the history of reprints is sometimes appalling—confirms, that they are read as the mainstream voices of American literature and are recognized as part of American popular culture. The marketability of the Jewish context attracted even certain non-Jewish writers to attempt Jewish subject matter in their fiction. Indisputably, the Jewish contribution to critical theory is even more commanding with the presence of Lionel Trilling, Harold Bloom, Irving Howe, Alfred Kazin, Leslie Fiedler—all of whom wrote on Jewish subject matter at one time or another. In the social sciences too, this trend continues. Sidney Hook, Daniel Bell, David Riesman, Philip Rahv, Norman Podhoretz, Irving Kristol and Nathan Glazer interpreted the American social situation—and the list could very easily be extended. Their political stance is wide and varied consisting of liberal, neo-conservative, Marxist and socialist views. Victor Navasky is the editor of the liberal *Nation,* while Podhoretz is a neo-conservative editing *Commentary,* a magazine sponsored by the American Jewish Committee. The editorial board of *Partisan Review*, a journal of a consistently high intellectual reputation, is heavily represented by Jewish intellectuals. Evidently, almost all of them pondered over issues concerning Jews at one point of their career and critically interpreted America for Americans as well as for the world.

The contribution of Jews of the American theatre, on the other hand, deserves a major recognition. American comedy can be conveniently called Jewish American comedy without running into any contradictions, for it has been consistently nurtured and nourished by Jewish playwrights over the years, starting from David Belasco of the early American theatre to Neil Simon. The inherent comic genius of the Jews, though it may appear unconventional in their thematic presentation, certainly drew them spontaneously to this mode of theatre. Considering the master craftsmanship and popularity of the writers of various critical acclaim, their achievement is laudable. Saul Bellow's *The Last Analysis* (1962, 1965), Woody Allen's intellectual comedy, Jules Feiffer's philosophical vaudeville *Knock Knock* (1976), among others, and Bruce Jay Friedman's black humour plays offer their range of perception and techniques. Even so, they gave a particular human dimension and supplemented it with a humanistic vision to the comic rhetoric. The assessment of Jewish American playwrights and their themes and techniques in the preceding pages prove sufficiently their stature in the American theatre. Harold Clurman, while generally talking about Yiddish influence on the American theatre, reemphasizes what Clive Barnes said regarding the Jewish patronage, that "if the Jews didn't go to plays in New York, there'd be Yom Kippur every night in the theatre."[15] Theatre criticism in America, which is a difficult profession by any assessment, has reached a new dimension with the contribution of George Jean Nathan, Harold Clurman and Robert Brustein.

The issues discussed so far give an unmistakable impression of Jewish excellence in various disciplines and definitely in the American theatre. While it is easy to enumerate their artistic achievements, one would do well to recognize the human factor they are always enthusiastic to introduce in whatever field they choose to practice or in whatever form or stance they profess to embrace. Whatever may be their proclamations or uneasiness towards their Jewishness, their attitude and their need to look for, and if possible to replace the existing society with, a better and more just world is in itself a central focus of Jewish sensibility. David Daiches expounding the necessity of explaining the nature of being Jewish as a universal paradigm, proposes an axiomatic view: "To emphasize one's Jewishness may be, in this environment, to emphasize one's sensibility, one's awareness of the intractability of human destiny. One's refusal to subscribe to any facile optimism about the rapid movement of modern industrial democratic society to Utopia, one's involvement in the contradictions and paradoxes of human nature."[16] Whether they choose to emphasize their Jewishness or not, their very affirmation or avoidance of the Jewish situation has, in a different way, brought them to the Jewish tradition, for their very espousal of human cause and universalism in lieu of parochialism echo Hebraic strain in more ways than one. To be sure, their endeavour, arguably, explains the rationality of their messianic favour that increasingly received the approval of the mainstream to the extent of making them the prophets of post-Enlightenment era.

NOTES

1. Joseph Mersand, *Traditions in American Literature* (New York: Kennikat Press, 1939), p. 1.
2. Irving Malin, *Jews and Americans* (Carbondale: Southern Illinois University Press, 1965), p. 4. Malin in this useful book comments on, among other aspects, the secular posture of Jews. Life in America is different from that of European shtetls where Jewishness reflected in every pattern of their existence. Jews never felt any cultural conflict. Living in America, being exposed to the gentile social milieu, he not only yearned to be accepted by the mainstream social structure but also made a gesture of coming to terms with it. The historical mission of a "bearer God's message" and "religious commitment" got replaced by social gospel, for it, while facilitating his quest for social acceptance, would also fulfil the messianic dream for a just society.

3. Lionel Trilling, "Under Forty," *The Literature of American Jews*, ed. Theodore Gross (New York: The Free Press, 1973), p. 360.
4. *Ibid.*
5. Lionel Trilling. "Wordsworth and the Rabbis," *The Opposing Self* (New York: The Viking Press, 1955). Taking a cue from Prof. Fairchild's argument in the third volume of his *Religious Trends in English Poetry* where he declares that Wordsworth's Christianity is dangerous since it lacks in "dogmatic principle" though it confirms to the social and ethical aspects of Christianity, Trilling argues that if Wordsworth is disliked by the Christian thinkers it is not entirely due to the absence of Christianity in his poetry but because he has affinity with an element—Judaic element—which is "not at the present time of chief importance to Christian intellectuals." (123) With this point made clear, he takes up the task of interpreting his poetry, establishing a parallel between the Law and Wordsworth's understanding of nature. In this attempt, he is largely guided by a book of sayings called *Pirke Aboth* edited by Rabbi Jehuda the Prince. However, Trilling's argument in this context did not seem to convince David Daiches who in an article called "Breakthrough?" (in *Contemporary Jewish American Literature*, ed. Irving Malin) believes that "the analogies are forced and the whole argument strained; it reads to me like something he really discovered." (34) If Daiches's view that Trilling "wanted to make himself believe" is plausible, it surely is a great transition from his earlier comments, which, it appears, is prototypal of many Jewish writers who had grumbled initially at the topic of Jewishness but later gleefully become affirmative.
6. Lionel Trilling. "The Changing Myth of the Jew," *Speaking of Literature and Society* (New York: Harcourt Brace Jovanovich, 1980).
7. Isaac Rosenfeld. "The Situation of the Jewish Writer," *An Age of Enormity: Life and Writing in the Forties and Fifties* (Cleveland: World, 1962), p. 69
8. Jacob Minkin, "The Jewish Book," *Mid-Century: An Anthology of Jewish Life and Culture in Our Times* (New York: The Becchburnt Press, 1955), p. 312.
9. Herman Wouk, "Why I Wrote a Jewish Novel," in *Mid-Century*, p. 326.
10. Irving Feldman, "Jewishness: Young Intellectuals," *Commentary* (April, 1961), p. 321.

11. Norman Podhoretz, *Commentary,* Vol. 31, No. 4 (April, 1961), p. 307.
12. Leslie and Joyce Field, "An Interview with Bernard Malamud" in *Bernard Malamud: A Collection of Critical Essays* (Englewood Cliffs, New Jersey: Prentice-Hall, 1975), p. 12.
13. Abraham Rothberg, "The Dilemma of the Jewish Writer," *Mid-Century*, p. 333.
14. Harold Bloom, *The Figures Capable of Imagination* (New York: The Seabury Press, 1976), p. 262.
15. Harold Clurman, *Creators and Disturbers* (New York: Columbia University Press, 1982), p. 177.
16. David Daiches, "Breakthrough?," *Contemporary American Jewish Literature,* ed. Irving Malin (Bloomington: Indiana University Press, 1973), p. 32.

BIBLIOGRAPHY

Primary Sources

Allen, Woody. *Play it Again, Sam. Best American Plays: Seventh Series 1967-1973.* New York: Crown Publishers, 1975.

Behrman, S.N. *Jacobowsky and the Colonel. The Best Plays of 1943-44.* New York: Dodd, Mead, 1944.

Belasco, David. *Men and Women. America's Lost Plays, XVIII.* Bloomington: Indiana University Press, 1940, 1965.

Chayefsky, Paddy. *Gideon.* New York: Random House, 1961.

------. *Middle of the Night.* New York: Random House, 1964.

------. *The Tenth Man.* New York: Random House, 1960.

Connelly, Marc. *The Green Pastures.* New York: Farrar and Rinehart, 1930.

Cumberland, Richard. *The Jew: A Comedy.* London, 1975.

Delbo, Charlotte. *Who Will Carry the Word? The Theatre of the Holocaust.* Wisconsin: The University of Wisconsin Press, 1982.

Feiffer, Jules. *Knock Knock.* New York: Hill and Wang, 1976.

Friedman, Bruce Jay. *Steambath. The Best Plays of* 1970-71. New York: Dodd, Mead, 1971.

Goodrich, Frances and Hackett, Albert. *The Diary of Anne Frank.* New York: Random House, 1956.

Heller, Joseph. *Claringer's Trial. The Best Short Plays (BSP) of 1976.* Pennsylvania: Chilton, 1976.

Hellman, Lillian, *Days to Come.* New York: Alfred A. Knopf, 1936.

------. *The Searching Wind.* New York: Viking, 1944

------. *Watch on the Rhine.* New York: Random, 1941.

------. *Scoundrel Time.* Boston: Little, Brown, 1976.

Hochhuth, Rolf. *The Deputy. Best Plays (BP) of 1963-64.* New York: Dodd, 1964.

Horowitz, Israel. *Stage Directions. The BSP of 1977.* Pennsylvania: Chilton, 1977.

------. *The Former One-on-One Basketball Champion. The BSP of 1981.*

Pennsylvania: Chilton, 1981.
------. *The Indian Wants the Bronx. The BSP of1969.* New York: Chilton, 1969.
Kassin, Michael. *To-day a Little Extra. The BSP of 1982.* Pennsylvania: Chilton, 1982.
Kaufman, Georg and Hart, Moss. *The American Way. Six Plays.* New York: The Modern Library, 1942, 1958.
Kirkland, Jack. *Tobacco Road. The Most Popular Plays of the American Theatre.* New York: Stein and Day, 1979, pp. 89-158.
Lessing, Gotthold Ephraim. *Nathan the Wise.* New York: Block Publishing, 1917.
Lewisohn, Ludwig. *Adam.* New York: Harper, 1929.
Lieberman, Harold and Edith. *Throne of Straw. The Theatre of the Holocaust,* 1982
Lifson, David S. *Epic and Folk Plays of the Yiddish Theatre.* Madison: Fairleigh Dickinson University Press, 1975.
Mc Leish, Archibald. *J.B.* Boston: Houghton Mifflin, 1956, 1958.
------. *Nobodaddy. Six Plays.* Houghton, 1980.
Mamet, David. *American Buffalo.* New York: Grover Press, 1976.
------. *A Life in the Theatre.* New York: Grover, 1977.
------. *Reunion and Dark Pony.* New York: Grover, 1979.
------. *Glengarry Glenross.* New York: Grover, 1984.
------. *Sexual Perversity in Chicago* and *Duck Variations.* New York: Grover, 1974.
Miller, Arthur. *Collected Plays.* New York: Viking Press, 1957, 1977.
------. *Collected Plays,* Vol. 11. New York: The Viking Press, 1981.
Nemerov, Howard. *The Collected Poems.* Chicago: The University of Chicago Press, 1977.
Nichols, Anne. *Abie's Irish Rose. The Most Popular Plays of the American Theatre.* New York: Stein and Day, 1979.
Odets, Clifford. *Six Plays.* New York: Random, 1939.
------. *The Big Knife.* New York: Random, 1949.
------. *The Flowering Peach,* a typescript available at ASRC, Hyderabad.
------. *Night Music.* New York: Random, 1940.
Owens, Rochelle. *The Karl Marx Play. The BSP of 1971.* Radnor, Pa: Chilton, 1971.
Ribman, Ronald. *Five Plays.* New York: Avon, 1978.
Rice, Elmer. *Flight to the West.* New York: Cowan-McCann, 1940, 1941.
Schary, Dore. *The Devil's Advocate.* New York: William Marrow, 1961.
Schisgal, Murray. *Pushcart Peddlers. The BSP of 1981.* Pennsylvania:

Chilton, 1981.
Schwartz, Joel. *Two Psalms of David. Playwrights for Tomorrow*, Vol. 9. Minneapolis: The University of Minneapolis, 1972.
Shakespeare, William. *The Merchant of Venice. The Complete Works of William Shakespeare*. Oxford, 1957.
Shaw, Robert. *The Man in the Glass Booth. The BP of 1968-69*. New York: Dodd, Mead, 1969.
Sherwood, Robert E. *Abe Lincoln in Illinois*. New York: Charles Scribner's Sons, 1937, 1939.
Simon, Neil. *The Comedy of Neil Simon*. New York: Random, 1979.
------. *The Collected Plays of Neil Simon*. Vol. 11. New York: Random, 1979.
------. *The Sunshine Boys*. New York: Random, 1973.
------. *The Odd Couple*. New York: Random, 1966.
------. *Brighton Beach Memoir*. New York: Random, 1984.
Stavis, Barrie. *Coat of Many Colors*. New York: A.S. Barnes, 1968.
Tabori, Georg. *The Cannibals. The Theatre of the Holocaust*, 1982.
Tyler, Royall. *The Judgement of Solomon. America's Lost Plays*, XV. Bloomington: Indiana University Press, 1940, 1965.
------. *The Origin of the Feast of Purim. America's Lost Plays*, XV, 1965.
------. *Joseph and His Brethren. America's Lost Plays*, XV.
------. *The Contrast. Dramas From the American Theatre*. Ed. Moody, Richard. Boston: Houghton Mifflin, 1966.
Udoff, Yale M. *The Little Gentleman. The BSP of 1971*. Pennsylvania: Chilton, 1971.
Weiss, Peter. *The Investigation*. New York: Atheneum, 1966.
Wesker, Arnold. *The Merchant*. London: Methuen, 1977, 1983.
Wilson, Lanford. *Talley's Folly*. New York: Hill and Wang, 1979.
Wincelberg, Shimon. *Resort 76. The Theatre of the Holocaust*, 1982.
Wouk, Herman. *The Cain Mutiny Court-Martial*. New York: Doubleday, 1954.
Zangwill, Israel. *The Melting Pot*. New York: MacMillan, 1909.

Secondary Sources

Aaron, Daniel. *Writers on the Left*. New York: Harcourt, 1961.
Adorno, T.W. et al. *The Authoritarian Personality*. New York: Harper and Row, 1950.
Antin, Mary. *The Promised Land*. New York: Houghton Mifflin, 1912.

Arendt, Hannah. *Eichmann in Jerusalem.* New York: Viking, 1975, C. 1965.

Baeck, Leo. *Jew and Christianity.* Philadelphia: Jewish Publication Society of America, 1958.

Bettelheim, Bruno. *Social Change and Prejudice.* New York: Free Press, 1950.

Bloom, Alexander. *Prodigal Songs: The New York Intellectuals and Their World.* New York: Oxford, 1986.

Bloom, Harold. *The Figures of Capable Imagination.* New York: The Scabury Press, 1976.

Bram, Robert A. *Elie Wiesel: Messenger to All Humanity.* Notre Dame: University of Notre Dame Press, 1983.

Brasch, Rudolph. *The Judaic Heritage: Its Teachings, Philosophy, and Symbols.* New York: Mckay, 1969.

Brenman-Gibson, Margaret. *Clifford Odets.* New York: Atheneum, 1982.

Brustein, Robert. "All Hail, Mahomet of Middle Seriousness." *New Republic*, Vol. 145. Nov. 27, 1961.

Cahan, Abraham, *The Rise of David Levinsky.* New York: Harper, 1917, rpt. 1960.

Clurman, Harold. *The Fervent Years.* New York: Harcourt Brace, 1945, 1975.

Crossman, Richard. *The God That Failed.* New York: Harper and Row, 1944, 1945.

Doctorow, E.L. *The Book of Daniel.* New York: New American Library, 1971, 1972.

Edward, Paul, ed. *Encyclopaedia Britannica,* Vol. 11. London: William Benton, 1929, 1961.

------. *Encylopaedia of Philosophy.* New York: The Macmillan, 1967.

Feingold, Henry L. *Zion in America: The Jewish-Experience from Colonial Times to Present.* New York: Twayne, 1974.

Feldman, Irving. "Jewishness and Young Intellectuals." *Commentary.* April, 1961.

Fiedler, Leslie. *To the Gentiles.* New York: Stein and Day, 1971.

Field, Leslie and Joyce. *Bernard Malamud: A Collection of Critical Essays.* Englewood Cliffs, New Jersey: Prentice-Hall, 1975.

Freud, Sigmund. *Jokes and Their Relation to the Unconscious.* London: Penguin, 1916, 1986.

Friedman, Lee Max. *Early American Jews.* Cambridge: Harvard, 1934.

Fromm, Erich. *You Shall Be As Gods.* New York: Holt, 1967, 1966.

Glazer, Nathan. *American Judaism.* Chicago: University of Chicago Press, 1957.

Gordis, Robert. *Judaism for the Modern Age.* New York: Farrar, 1955.

Gross, Theodore L. ed. *The Literature of American Jews.* New York: Free Press, 1973.

Guttmann, Allen. *The Jewish Writer in America: Assimilation and the Crisis of Identity.* New York: Oxford University Press, 1971.

Handlin, Oscar. *The Uprooted.* New York: Little Brown, 1952.

Harap, Louis. *The Image of the Jew in American Literature.* Philadelphia: The Jewish Publication Society in America, 1974.

Heilbut, Anthony. *Exiled in Paradise; German Refugee Artists and Intellectuals in America, from the 1930s to the Present.* New York: Viking, 1983.

Hellman, Lillian. *Three.* Boston: Little, Brown, 1979.

Heschel, Abraham Joshua. *The Earth is the Lord's* and *Sabbath.* Cleveland: World, 1963.

Hilberg, Raul. *Destruction of the European Jews.* New York: Quadrangle Books, 1961.

Howe, Irving and Greenberg, Eliezer, ed. *Ashes Out of Hope.* New York: Schocken, 1977.

------. *A Margin of Hope: An Intellectual Autobiography.* New York: Harcourt, 1982.

Huber, Richard M. *The American Idea of Success.* New York: McGraw, 1971.

Kafka, Franz. *The Complete Stories.* Ed. Glatzer, Nahum. New York: Schocken, 1971.

Kauffmann, Stanley. *Person of the Drama.* New York: Harper and Row, 1967, 1976.

Knopp, Josephine Z. *The Trial of Judaism in Contemporary Jewish Writing.* Urbana: University of Illinois Press, 1975.

Koestler, Arthur. *Darkness at Noon.* New York: Time, 1962.

Kurtz, Paul. *The Humanist Alternative: Some Definitions of Humanism.* New York: Prometheus Books, 1974.

Lewisohn, Ludwig. *The Last Days of Shylock.* New York: Harper, 1931.

Liebman, Arthur. *Jews and the Left.* New York: Wiley, 1979.

Lippmann, Walter. *Public Opinion.* New York: Free Press, 1922.

Liptzin, Soloman. *The Jew in American Literature.* New York: Block, 1966.

Maimonides, Moses. *Guide of the Perplexed.* London: East and West Library, 1952.

Malin, Irving. *Jews and Americans.* Carbondale: Southern Illinois University Press, 1965.

------, ed. *Contemporary American Jewish Literature.* Bloomington: Indiana University Press, 1973.

Marcus, Jacob. *The Jew in Medieval World.* New York: A Temple Book, 1983.

------, ed. *American Jews; documents of eighteenth century; primarily hitherto unpublished manuscripts.* Cincinnati: Hebrew Union College Press, 1959.

Martine, James. "Miller's Roots and His Moral Dilemma" or "Continuity from Brooklyn to *Salesman.*" *Critical Essays: Arthur Miller.* Ed. Martine, James. Boston: G.K. Hall, 1979.

Mayer, Hans. *Outsiders; a study in Life and Letters.* Cambridge, Mass.: MIT Press, 1984, 1982.

Mendes-Flohr, Paul and Reinharz Jehuda. *The Jew in the Modern World.* New York: Oxford, 1980.

McCarthy, Mary. *Venice Observed.* London: Heinemann, 1956, 1961.

McGovern, Edythe M. *Neil Simon: A Critical Study.* New York: Frederick Unger, 1978.

Mersand, Joseph. *Tradition in American Literature: a Study of Jewish Characters and Authors.* New York: Kenniket Press, 1968, C. 1939.

Miller, Arthur. *The Theatre Essays of Arthur Miller.* New York: Viking, 1978.

Nolan, Paul, T. *Marc Connelly.* New York: Twayne, 1969.

Patai, Raphael. *On Jewish Folkore.* Detroit: Wayne University Press, 1983.

Pawel, Ernst. *New York Times Book Review.* Feb. 20, 1984.

Pinsker, Sanford Sigmund. *The Schlemiel as Metaphor: Studies in Yiddish and American Jewish Novel.* Ph.D. thesis submitted to University of Washington, 1967. Microfilm.

Podhoretz, Norman. *Commentary.* Vol. 31, No. 4, April, 1961.

Prior, Moody E. "Which Is the Jew that Shakespeare Drew." *The American Scholar.* Autumn, 1981.

Rabkin, Gerald. *Drama and Commitment.* Bloomington: Indiana University Press, 1964.

Reik, Theodor. *Jewish Wit.* New York: Gamut Press, 1962.

Ribalow, Harold U. *Mid-Century: an Anthology of Jewish Life and Authors in Our Times.* New York: Beechurst Press, 1955.

Richard, Stanley. "Introduction." *The Most Popular Plays of the Ameri-*

can Theatre. New York: Stein and Day, 1979.

Rosenberg, Bernard and Goldstein, Ernest. *Creators and Disturbers*. New York: Columbia, 1982.

Rosenberg, Edgar. *From Shylock to Svengali; Jewish Stereotypes in European Fiction*. Stanford, California: Stanford University Press, 1960.

Rosenfeld, Alving H. *Confronting the Holocaust*. Bloomington: Indiana University Press, 1978.

Rosenfeld, Isaac. *An Age of Enormity*. Cleveland: World, 1962.

Roskies, David. G. *Against the Apocalypse: Responses to Catastrophe in Modern Jewish Culture*. Cambridge, Mass.: Harvard University Press, 1984.

Roth, Philip. *Portnoy's Complaint*. London: Jonathan Cape, 1969.

Schiff, Ellen. *From Stereotype to Metaphor; the Jews in Contemporary Drama*. New York: SUNY Press, 1982.

Sevell, Max. *Is Liberalism Dead?* Seattle: University of Washington Press, 1967.

Sills, David, ed. *International Encyclopaedia of the Social Sciences*. New York: The Macmillan, 1968.

Steiner, George. *In Bluebeard's Castle: Some Notes Towards the Redefinition of Culture*. London: Faber and Faber, 1971.

------. *Language and Silence; Essays on Language, Literature and the Inhuman*. New York: Atheneum, 1967.

------. *The Death of Tragedy*. London: Faber, 1961.

Strauss, Leo. *Liberalism: Ancient and Modern*. New York: Basic Books, 1968.

Taubman, Howard. "A Proper God," *Time*. Nov. 17, 1961.

Trachtenberg, Joshua. *The Devil and the Jew*. New York: Meridian, 1943.

Trilling, Lionel. *Speaking of Literature and Society*. New York: Harcourt, 1980.

------. *The Opposing Self*. New York: The Viking, 1955.

Updike, John. *Bech: A Book*. London: Andre Deutsch, 1970.

------. *Bech Is Back*. New York: Alfred A. Knopf, 1982.

Weales, Gerald. *Clifford Odets: Playwright*. New York: Pegasus, 1971.

Wheeler, Thomas, ed. *The Immigrant Experience*. Baltimore: Penguin, 1971.

Wisse, Ruth R. *The Schlemiel as Modern Hero*. Chicago: University of Chicago Press, 1971.

Zatlin, Linda Gestner. *The Nineteenth Century Anglo-Jewish Novel*. Boston: Twayne, 1981.

Index